Lecture Notes in Computer Science   12220

More information about this series at http://www.springer.com/series/7409

Sara Hofmann · Csaba Csáki ·
Noella Edelmann · Thomas Lampoltshammer ·
Ulf Melin · Peter Parycek ·
Gerhard Schwabe · Efthimios Tambouris (Eds.)

Electronic Participation

12th IFIP WG 8.5 International Conference, ePart 2020
Linköping, Sweden, August 31 – September 2, 2020
Proceedings

 Springer

Editors
Sara Hofmann ⓘ
University of Agder
Kristiansand, Norway

Noella Edelmann ⓘ
Danube University Krems
Krems, Austria

Ulf Melin ⓘ
Linköping University
Linköping, Sweden

Gerhard Schwabe
University of Zurich
Zurich, Switzerland

Csaba Csáki ⓘ
Corvinus University of Budapest
Budapest, Hungary

Thomas Lampoltshammer ⓘ
Danube University Krems
Krems, Austria

Peter Parycek ⓘ
Danube University Krems
Krems, Austria

Efthimios Tambouris ⓘ
University of Macedonia
Thessaloniki, Greece

ISSN 0302-9743   ISSN 1611-3349   (electronic)
Lecture Notes in Computer Science
ISBN 978-3-030-58140-4   ISBN 978-3-030-58141-1   (eBook)
https://doi.org/10.1007/978-3-030-58141-1

LNCS Sublibrary: SL3 – Information Systems and Applications, incl. Internet/Web, and HCI

This Springer imprint is published by the registered company Springer Nature Switzerland AG
The registered company address is: Gewerbestrasse 11, 6330 Cham, Switzerland

Preface

Welcome to the third joint EGOV-CeDEM-ePart 2020! The conference presents the merger of the IFIP WG 8.5 Electronic Government (EGOV), the IFIP WG 8.5 Electronic Participation (ePart), and the E-Democracy and Open Government Conference (CeDEM). The conference is a well-known international venue for exchanging ideas among researchers and also practitioners in the field of e-Government, Open Government, eParticipation, and e-Democracy, as well as the role of social media, digital transformation in society, artificial intelligence, policy information, smart governance, and social innovation.

This year's preparation and execution of the conference have been heavily influenced by the COVID-19 pandemic. Originally planned to take place at Linköping University in Sweden, EGOV-CeDEM-ePart 2020 was held as a fully digital conference during August 31 – September 2. The authors recorded a short presentation of their paper beforehand so that during the conference the focus was on providing feedback, discussion, and learning from each other. While we lost some of the ad-hoc meetings and informal gatherings, we managed to have much interaction and participation.

EGOV-CeDEM-ePart 2020 attracted different types of submissions, including completed research, ongoing research, practitioner papers, reflections and viewpoints, posters, and workshops. In addition, the conference organized a PhD colloquium. EGOV-CeDEM-ePart welcomes individuals from academic and applied backgrounds as well as from business, public authorities, NGOs, NPOs, and education institutions. The submissions are distributed over the following tracks:

- General e-Government & e-Governance Track
- General e-Democracy & e-Participation Track
- AI, Data Analytics & Automated Decision Making Track
- Smart Cities (Government, Communities & Regions) Track
- Social Media Track
- Social Innovation Track
- Open Data: Social and Technical Aspects Track
- Digital Society Track
- Cybersecurity Track
- Legal Informatics Track
- Practitioners' Track

The ePart proceedings contain 11 completed research papers, which accounts for an acceptance rate of 33%. The papers are distributed among the General e-Democracy & e-Participation, Social Media, Legal Informatics, Digital Society, and Social Innovation tracks. Another 30 completed research papers are included in the LNCS EGOV proceedings (vol. 12219).

The volume starts with eParticipation Developments and the case of a district authority in Hungary that decided to build an eParticipation program from scratch presented by Csaba Csáki. He unveils challenges of using digital technologies in extended democratic decision making. Joachim Åström and Martin Karlsson take on a new perspective of trust research in eParticipation. They analyze Swedish public managers' trust in citizens when collaborating with them in participation projects.

In the area of Digital Transformation, Efthimios Tambouris and Epameinondas Troulinos investigate the transformation of information systems in the jurisdiction. They explore how the governance structure of the Integrated Administrative Court Case Management System of Greece has affected the decisions regarding interoperability. Nitesh Bharosa, Silvia Lips, and Dirk Draheim analyze data exchange infrastructures, which are needed for transforming the public sector. In doing so, they compare the different approaches in The Netherlands and in Estonia. A more theoretical perspective on digital transformation is taken by Thomas Vogl. He discusses diverse perspectives to the study of technologically supported social innovation in the public sector.

Two papers deal with Open Government and Transparency. Noella Edelmann and Mary Francoli explore the connection between a government's membership in the Open Government Partnership initiative and their digital transformation. Another perspective of openness is pursued by Changwoo Suh, Byungtae Lee, Habin Lee, Youngseok Choi, and Sunghan Ryu. In their contribution, they identify what attributes of online games need to be disclosed to the market for policy makers.

Several papers in our volume consider the User Perspective. Charalampos Alexopoulos, Shefali Virkar, Michalis Avgerinos Loutsaris, Anna-Sophie Novak, and Euripidis Loukis analyze how to design effective and useful systems for the provision of legal information. In this context, they identify the legal information requirements of designers of public policies. Mariana S. Gustafsson, Elin Wihlborg, and Johanna Sefyrin consider the concept of citizenship and how it is mediated by technology. Their findings are based on a field study in Swedish libraries where they examine how citizenship is practiced in an advanced digital society. Karin Skill and Ahmed Kaharevic also consider the Swedish context. They explore digital participation and inclusion in eHealth in a marginalized neighborhood. The volume closes with a study on chatbots in public agencies. Linett Simonsen, Tina Steinstø, Guri Verne, and Tone Bratteteig present their findings from chat logs and identify different types of lack of domain knowledge.

We would like to thank all the contributors who have aided in making this year's conference a success. Our gratitude goes to the track chairs, the members of the Program Committee and the additional reviewers for their effort in preparing the conference as well as reviewing and selecting the accepted papers, and to the authors for submitting their papers. A special thanks goes to the local organizers at Linköping University for their preparation and their flexibility in these challenging times. The conference was only possible with the help and contribution from all of you.

August 2020

Sara Hofmann
Csaba Csáki
Noella Edelmann
Thomas Lampoltshammer
Ulf Melin
Peter Parycek
Gerhard Schwabe
Efthimios Tambouris

Organization

Conference Lead Organizer

Marijn Janssen   Delft University of Technology, The Netherlands

General e-Government and e-Governance Track

Gabriela Viale Pereira   Danube University Krems, Austria
Ida Lindgren   Linköping University, Sweden
Hans Jochen Scholl   University of Washington, USA

General e-Democracy and e-Participation Track

Noella Edelmann   Danube University Krems, Austria
Peter Parycek   Danube University Krems, Austria
Robert Krimmer   Tallinn University of Technology, Estonia

Smart Cities (Government, Communities and Regions) Track

Manuel Pedro Rodríguez   University of Granada, Spain
    Bolívar
Karin Axelsson   Linköping University, Sweden
Nuno Lopes   DTx: Digital Transformation CoLab, Portugal

AI, Data Analytics and Automated Decision Making Track

Habin Lee   Brunel University London, UK
Euripidis Loukis   University of the Aegean, Greece
Evangelos Kalampokis   University of Macedonia, Greece

Social Media Track

Sara Hofmann   University of Agder, Norway
Marius Rohde Johannessen   University of South-Eastern Norway, Norway
Panos Panagiotopoulos   Queen Mary University of London, UK

Social Innovation Track

Csaba Csáki   Corvinus University of Budapest, Hungary
Gianluca Misuraca   European Commission's Joint Research Centre, Spain
Marijn Janssen   Delft University of Technology, The Netherlands

Open Data: Social and Technical Aspects Track

Anneke Zuiderwijk   Delft University of Technology, The Netherlands
Ramon Gil-Garcia   University at Albany, SUNY, USA
Efthimios Tambouris   University of Macedonia, Greece

Digital Society Track

Thomas Lampoltshammer   Danube University Krems, Austria
Christian Østergaard   IT University of Copenhagen, Denmark
  Madsen
Katarina L. Gidlund   Mid Sweden University, Sweden

Cybersecurity Track

Natalia Kadenko   Delft University of Technology, The Netherlands
Marijn Janssen   Delft University of Technology, The Netherlands

Legal Informatics Track

Peter Parycek   Danube University Krems, Austria
Anna-Sophie Novak   Danube University Krems, Austria

Practitioners' Track

Francesco Mureddu   The Lisbon Council, Belgium
Peter Reichstädter   Austrian Parliament, Austria
Francesco Molinari   Politecnico di Milano, Italy
Morten Meyerhoff Nielsen   United Nations University, Portugal

Chair of Outstanding Papers Awards

Noella Edelmann   Danube University Krems, Austria
Evangelos Kalampokis   University of Macedonia, Greece

PhD Colloquium Chairs

Gabriela Viale Pereira   Danube University Krems, Austria
J. Ramon Gil-Garcia   University at Albany, SUNY, USA
Ida Lindgren   Linköping University, Sweden

Program Committee

Suha Alawadhi   Kuwait University, Kuwait
Karin Ahlin   Mid Sweden University, Sweden
Valerie Albrecht   Danube University Krems, Austria

Jeremy Millard	Third Millennium Governance, Denmark
Yuri Misnikov	University of Leeds, UK
Gianluca Misuraca	European Commission's Joint Research Centre, Belgium
Francesco Molinari	University of Rijeka, Croatia
Francesco Mureddu	Lisbon Council, Portugal
Michael Möstl	Danube University Krems, Austria
Alessia Caterina Neuroni	Bern University of Applied Sciences, Switzerland
Hanne-Westh Nicolajsen	IT University of Copenhagen, Denmark
Mille Nielsen	IT University of Copenhagen, Denmark
Peter Axel Nielsen	Aalborg University, Denmark
Anastasija Ņikiforova	University of Latvia, Latvia
Anna-Sophie Novak	Danube University Krems, Austria
Panos Panagiotopoulos	Queen Mary University of London, UK
Darcy Parks	Linköping University, Sweden
Peter Parycek	Danube University Krems, Austria
Sergio Picazo-Vela	Universidad de las Americas Puebla, Mexico
Sofie Pileman	Linköping University, Sweden
Luiz Pereira Pinheiro Junior	Universidade Positivo, Brazil
Kerley Pires	United Nations University, Portugal
Florin Pop	University Politehnica of Bucharest, Hungary
Anisah Herdiyanti Prabowo	Delft University of Technology, The Netherlands
Peter Reichstädter	Austrian Parliament, Austria
Nicolau Reinhard	University of São Paulo, Brazil
Taiane Ritta Coelho	Federal University of Parana, Brazil
A. Paula Rodríguez Müller	KU Leuven, Belgium
Manuel Pedro Rodríguez Bolívar	University of Granada, Spain
Alexander Ronzhyn	University of Koblenz-Landau, Germany
Athanasia Routzouni	University of the Aegean, Greece
Boriana Rukanova	Delft University of Technology, The Netherlands
Per Runeson	Lund University, Sweden
Michael Räckers	University of Münster, Germany
Rodrigo Sandoval-Almazan	Universidad Autonoma del Estado de Mexico, Mexico
Günter Schefbeck	Austrian Parliament, Austria
Hans Jochen Scholl	University of Washington, USA
Hendrik Scholta	University of Münster, Germany
Harrie Scholtens	European Institute of Public Administration, The Netherlands
Johannes Scholz	Graz University of Technology, Austria
Judith Schossböck	Danube University Krems, Austria
Luiza Schuch de Azambuja	Tallinn University of Technology, Estonia
Erich Schweighofer	University of Vienna, Austria
Johanna Sefyrin	Linköping University, Sweden
Tobias Siebenlist	Heinrich Heine University Düsseldorf, Germany
Anthony Simonofski	KU Leuven, Belgium

Søren Skaarup	IT University of Copenhagen, Denmark
David Spacek	Masaryk University, Czech Republic
Vera Spitzer	University of Koblenz-Landau, Germany
Karin Steiner	Danube University Krems, Austria
Leif Sundberg	Mid Sweden University, Sweden
Iryna Susha	Örebro University, Sweden
Proscovia Svärd	Mid Sweden University, Sweden
Øystein Sæbø	University of Agder, Norway
Fredrik Söderström	Linköpings University, Sweden
Efthimios Tambouris	University of Macedonia, Greece
Aurelia Tamo-Larrieux	University of Zurich, Switzerland
Luca Tangi	Politecnico di Milano, Italy
Konstantinos Tarabanis	University of Macedonia, Greece
Luis Terán	University of Fribourg, Switzerland
Lörinc Thurnay	Danube University Krems, Austria
Jolien Ubacht	Delft University of Technology, The Netherlands
Mathias Van Compernolle	Ghent University, Belgium
Sélinde van Engelenburg	Delft University of Technology, The Netherlands
Marco Velicogna	IRSIG-CNR, Italy
Gabriela Viale Pereira	Danube University Krems, Austria
Shefali Virkar	Danube University Krems, Austria
Cancan Wang	IT University of Copenhagen, Denmark
Frederika Welle Donker	Knowledge Centre Open Data, The Netherlands
Guilherme Wiedenhöft	Federal University of Rio Grande, Brazil
Elin Wihlborg	Linköping University, Sweden
Maija Ylinen	Tampere University of Technology, Finland
Chien-Chih Yu	National Cheng Chi University, China
Thomas Zefferer	A-SIT Plus GmbH, Austria
Qinfeng Zhu	University of Groningen, The Netherlands
Anneke Zuiderwijk	Delft University of Technology, The Netherlands

Additional Reviewers

Michele Benedetti	Silvia Lips
Yannis Charalabidis	Yu-lun Liu
Jaewon Choi	Auriane Marmier
Ruth Angelie Cruz	Claudio Russo
Alizée Francey	Janine Ulrich
Mariana Gustafsson	Colin van Noordt
Sangwook Ha	Gianluigi Viscusi
Karl Kristian Larsson	Dimitris Zeginis
Junyeong Lee	

Contents

eParticipation Developments

An Attempt to Build an eParticipation Program from Scratch: The Case of a District Municipality

Csaba Csáki(✉) 📵

Corvinus University of Budapest, Budapest, Hungary
csaki.csaba@uni-corvinus.hu

Abstract. The use of electronic tools to support the democratic process through inclusive participation has almost a two decades history - but not in all countries. There are regions where eParticipation projects are still in their infancy. Albeit there are mature "best practices", they mostly address issues faced by developed countries with strong tradition of democracy in general, where transition to online, technology based solution is on a normal trajectory. On the other hand, there is a growing collection of case studies from all over the world with very differing views on the option - and diverging needs how to proceed and how to make ePart projects successful. This paper reports on research that addressed technology related challenges a district authority in the capital of Hungary faced when decided to embark on a program of extended democratic decision making - with the possibility to utilize digital technologies.

Keywords: eParticipation · Deliberative democracy · Municipal government · Local democracy · Participation platform

1 Introduction

The ideal of inclusive deliberative democracy aims at greater public participation in political and administrative decision making, but it also requires appropriate channels, methods and tools for it to become a successful practice [2]. With the emergence of electronic government (eGov) on the back of the Internet, digital technology has become an option for citizen participation: eParticipation (ePart) now has a history of a bit over fifteen years [14]. Scientific interest in these areas have also increased. On the one hand, various theoretical frameworks have been proposed to analyze ePart projects (including evaluation models covering a set of criteria), on the other hand numerous case studies had been published offering critical success factors (CSF) and best practices how to run such projects [13, 18, 20, 23, 26].

Already in 2004 Macintosh warned [14], that at the start of an ePart project there is a need to *"clearly characterize the stage in the policy-making process, the level of participation, the technology used, and various issues and constraints, including the*

© IFIP International Federation for Information Processing 2020
Published by Springer Nature Switzerland AG 2020
S. Hofmann et al. (Eds.): ePart 2020, LNCS 12220, pp. 3–14, 2020.
https://doi.org/10.1007/978-3-030-58141-1_1

potential benefits online participation offers" (p. 2). Participation, however, is not a self-serving goal: eParticipations initiatives usually aim at creating a climate of transparency, trust and creative interaction in the government-citizen relationship using technology [18] which could bring benefits for both parties over the long run.

Although, there is a slowly growing set of practical evidence how to start such projects locally when there is no visible civic engagement and involvement of civil society in political matters is not welcomed by national politics (e.g. [10, 11, 28]), there appears to be no comprehensive summary of best ePart practice specifically addressed to newcomers who operate in a controversial political context. Such need has arisen when one of the campaign promises of the (opposition) coalition who won the local elections in one of the Districts of Budapest in October 2019 was to extend participation and open up the municipal decision making process. To translate their task into a research challenge the following (pragmatic) research objective was formulated: What practical advice may be concluded from ePart literature that could be used by a local municipality to strengthen participation in a climate of political division and general public apathy; and what strategy to follow regarding the utilization of technology.

This paper, reporting on the research that has ensued is organized as follows. First the case and its context is presented briefly to set the stage. The third section presents basic concepts and definitions of participatory democracy and electronic participation followed by a short review of tools applied and a brief overview of best practices and evaluation frameworks. This leads to our research questions and the methodology applied. The analysis of the case study focuses on questions faced and tools investigated followed by a detailed discussion of the findings and main messages. The paper is closed by a discussion of results and planned future work.

2   Introduction to the Case (as Research Motivation)

During the October 2019 local elections in one of the Districts of Budapest a coalition – formed mostly by opposition parties and civil organizations – won: they got the major position and majority in the municipal assembly. One of the campaign promises was to improve transparency and allow local residents more say in district matters. The goal of the new leadership was to extend participation, improve fairness, and open up the municipal decision making process including better access to information. They were determined to improve both width and depth of reach, funnel ideas from local civilians, and co-create selected policy (by allowing for involvement, discussion, and feedback). They intended to do participatory planning and design in revitalization of public places.

However, they had to face a deep political division, high level of nepotism by the outgoing office, and a general level of (political) apathy. There were only a few active individuals and NGOs backing their agenda. There were several ongoing planning projects drawing civil attention - albeit reactions had been mostly fueled by anger and motivated by frustration as important decisions were made without consultations. Civil engagement thus were mostly protest-based against the way city-level projects were planned and executed.

To improve participation the major's office planned to investigate options of ICT-based solutions. Our group was invited as eGov experts to help define the tasks ahead and offer best practices. As personal connections do matter, they needed to balance authority and legitimacy, while broadening public participation through gradually allowing more room for citizen control.

3 Participatory Democracy and Electronic Participation

3.1 Key Ideas Behind eParticipation with Focus on the Local Level

Participatory democracy is the broad participation of constituents in the direction-setting and operation of political systems [2]. There appears to be a need to open up representative democracy to achieve a higher involvement of civil society so people may bring their divergent views and interests to solve public issues [14]. Such participatory initiatives may be the results of top-down engagements, or may come from ground-up efforts where citizens seek empowerment in support of various causes [1]. However, inclusion of citizens and organizations requires new forums, methods and procedures [7] as all interested parties should have access to relevant data and be able to contribute. The expected outcome is not only a wider, yet well-informed debate (avoiding reliance on emotional arguments only), but also transparent decisions that may be better accepted [24]. From this point of view eParticipation – as part of eDemocracy along eVoting – is the use of information technology to support democratic decision-making [6]. ePart implies the use of info-communication technologies (ICT) to form innovative practices that enable various stakeholders to take part in policy making processes [4]. Main objectives of ePart include [17] broader participation and support of more efficient participation (by offering a selection of tools addressing citizen groups of differing technical and communication skills), and creating a well-informed deliberative debate in support of deeper contributions. This is expected to increase legitimacy and quality of the decision, whether concluded during the process or based on the input originated from the participatory initiative. Regarding participants the agreement in the literature is that the widest possible involvement of stakeholders would be ideal (spanning demographic groups and reaching out to civil organizations).

One arena where citizen participation in democratic decision-making processes can be realized with immediate visible results is local governments and municipalities (of different levels) [22]. The key is to allow citizens/residents to engage with the local political establishment in their decision-making processes affecting societal groups or involving issues of public interest in the given locality. ePart at the local level provides municipalities with ICT-based opportunities for consultation and dialogue while minimizing logistical and communication constraints associated with traditional engagement methods [21]. Booher [3] summarizes five reasons for the participation of citizens in municipal decision making: 1) information gathering: decision-makers can find out what the public's preferences are and consider them in their decisions; 2) local expertise: decisions can be improved by incorporating citizens' local knowledge; 3) democratic values: public participation can advance fairness and justice; 4) democratic process: public participation helps getting legitimacy for public decisions; 5) regulatory conformance: participation is offered by public officials because the law requires it (p. 422). However, there are reports and arguments that ePart initiatives did not always achieve a more participatory process [16] – or at least not automatically. Hepburn [8] warns of political challenges and the influence of vested economic interests local governments have to deal with. Consequently, if local governments intend to use electronic tools in order to strengthen local democracy they have to develop strategies to tackle such issues. They also have to prepare their organization through reformed internal processes and structure augmented with education that is prepared to enable and support local citizen-ship (including youth, social workers and NGOs) enacting their interests online [27]. They also need to choose fitting tools.

3.2 Tools of eParticipation

ICT-based participatory tools may take many forms from online petition, public opinion polls, surveys, or complaint portals to electronic discussion forums, online policy consul-tation projects or even talking to officials directly online [18]. General Internet solutions such as social media, Web portals, alert services, groupware tools, webcasts, wikis, pod-casts or blogs may also be utilized [26]; while on the other end of the spectrum there are dedicated complex platforms of deliberative participation developed (i.e. ourspace, yrpri.org, consul, b-involved, decidim). In judging the usefulness of any ePart tool one key characteristic is if it allows one way or two way communication or something in between (restricted two-way).

Regarding usability, some tools may fit certain purposes but could fail to support others. For example social media now has a wide reach and is good for information dispatch or mobilization (especially against something [21] and may even offer platform for discussion, but not fit for participation because people do not use it to express political opinion, arguments may become simplified and emotional, and it is questionable whether such positions would reach the administration. Opinions seem to converge that effective ePart programs that have a long term impact in mind should consider the use of a deliberative platform dedicated to give space to diverging opinions and help contradicting standpoints to reach a conclusion.

3.3 Theoretical and Evaluation Frameworks of eParticipation

Based on the main goals of eParticipation a number of descriptive models as well as analytical and evaluation frameworks have been proposed [25]. The layered model of Macintosh and Whyte [15] addresses three perspectives: democratic, project, and socio-technical – composed of 20 single evaluation criteria. The 7Ps of sustainable ePartici-pation implementation by Islam [9] covers policy and capacity building, planning and goal setting, programs and contents development, process and tools, promotion, partici-pation, and post-implementation analysis (in this order as they form a process, where the participation stage has its own internal steps). The participatory action research (PAR) model [1] simplifies the above into 5 stages for developing countries and accommodates both top-down and bottom-up initiation. However, Dahler-Larsen [5] points out that a too much program and process centered mindset can lead to neglect of the often complex interaction of these with their context. Evaluation frameworks offer a set of dimensions (such as fairness, competence, acceptance, quality of process etc.) covering a wide range of criteria (for reviews see [13, 18, or 20]).

As for unsupportive contexts, Kabanov and Chugunov [10] starts with the assumption that autocracies in general have ineffective institutional performance regarding civic relationships, then show that e-projects can still survive in case of local political patronage and may achieve some – albeit limited – institutional changes. Kneuer and Harnisch, [11] argue that while autocratic regimes may actually establish efficient web-based bureaucratic processes, they do so "*without institutionalized distributions of democratic powers to those affected*" (p. 550). Wakabi and Grönlund [28] show that low belief of citizens that they may influence change and fear of backlash limits their interest in e-Participation, and keeps them away from political matters.

4 Practical Research Questions and Methodology

Despite all these frameworks it is not straightforward how eParticipation projects should be initiated and how to take into consideration specific characteristics of local democracy and civic engagement, or lack thereof. This was the challenge local authorities in Hungary faced late 2019 (after civil organizations working with opposition parties have won local elections in several cities). To support the efforts of one capital district government the following research questions have been put forward: 1) What strategy may a local authority utilize to mobilize a wider constituency when they have to combat historical apathy? 2) What requirements follow against technological (ICT) support of the above goal? 3) What tool(s) would meet the expectations best and in what order tools/features/services/functions should be introduced?

This is essentially an exploratory qualitative case study using a mixture of data collection methods. Desk work included literature review on frameworks and cases in order to collect CSFs, and this was augmented with online search of potential ePart tools. Field work consisted of interviews with 4 municipal leaders and 4 participatory democracy experts, and observation of 4 participatory (face-to-face) forums to collect requirements. Interviews lasted approximately one hour each and formed of open ended questions, while at the forums detailed minutes were taken and citizen opinion was collected using a simple questionnaire. The conclusion was a report to the ePart officer regarding CSFs and an evaluation of potential solutions. Analysis was conducted based on this data and was contrasted with findings of the literature review.

5 Useful Literature: Critical Success Factors to Consider

The first step was to review preconditions of effective ePart projects and critical success factors in achieving a legitim process along with potential barriers. The structural model of participation initiatives by Kubicek and Aichholzer [12] offers CSFs to judge if there were strong links from the given project to formal political decision making. Panopoulou et al. [18] distil seven CSFs that makes a difference: commitment by the government; usability of tools; combining online with offline channels; a thorough communication and promotion plan; ensuring security and privacy; addressing organizational issues; and handling complexity of the topic and quality of participation. Smith et al. [26] claim that external factors (including the choice of technology, institutional setting, and elements of political and societal context) need to be carefully investigated as they may act either as drivers or barriers. Their main message is that eParticipation is essentially a relationship-building process. Consequently, the goals of participatory initiatives evolve from providing (building tools and offering methods) to using (utilizing the tools and methods available) to practicing (making it to be the norm to consider and integrate these solutions). Furthermore, *"it is necessary to identify the external factors in the environment within which a project exists and the wider processes with which it must co-exist"* (p. 310). Primus et al., [23] is a comprehensive example of best practice recommendations as it defines 36 CSFs along 6 dimensions. Based on a cross-cultural perspective Parycek et al. [20] offered the following lessons and CSFs: select topics carefully; integrate affected decision makers into the discussion, but also provide moderation (both on- and off-line with the intent that neither politicians nor expert should overdominate the discourse); manage community (especially for the long-run); use a mix of channels (augment the discussion tool with social media channels or even blogs carrying background information); offer social media features so participants can connect beyond the topic at hand (or could create links to such known services like user profiles or groups). Panopoulou et al. [19] proposed success factors specifically tailored for designing eParticipation initiatives, where each factor had a set of activities associated with them. Many of these factors, practices and barriers are reinforced by case studies (a good example is [27]).

6 Analysis: Conflicting Goals and Challenges Faced

Several of the issues raised by literature was indeed present in the district case. It was clear to municipal leaders that they need to make changes to internal rules along with reorganizing the structure and processes of the administration. But the success of these ongoing changes do depend on a deeper cultural change requiring education of staff. Such a sweeping change is not an ideal setting for initiating ePart projects - but more opportunities for participation and a wider access to municipal decision making was a major campaign promise that the major and elected officials were keen on keeping. The stake is also high, because in case of failure the desire to participate in future projects may meet resistance.

Based on the findings of the previous section the following CSFs were recommended: committed champion; prepared staff; mix of channels (in communication and participation alike); intuitive tool(s); careful selection of individual projects; detailed promotion and communications strategy of those projects; balance the level of privacy and the degree of anonymity allowed; managing the process; participant preparation; apply moderation for online discussions.

They have appointed a "participatory advisor" and our first task was to review current projects and existing communication channels as well as to collect requirements against ICT and compare them to potential ePart tool options. Most of the ongoing projects of civic engagement were planning activities, revitalization initiatives or policy related to traffic, parking, or regulating shop facades. They have also considered participatory budgeting but it was decided to delay it until later in the year (influencing budget of next year). For dissemination and engagement these ongoing projects utilized public displays at the local Old Market; email lists; Facebook posts; as well as community forums at the local cultural center. Also needed to rely on a few existing, active civil groups.

The solution had to support different phases of the participatory process (i.e.: 1) collect project ideas; 2) project selection; 3) promotion and dissemination of background information; 4) ideas, comments on solutions; 5) discussion, deliberation; 6) voting,; 7) implementation control; 8) feedback about results) and other activities (such as communication channels, authenticated registration, community building, links to social media, moderation, or special access for more senior officers). The divergent types of projects (above) posed a wide range of challenges as each had different target audience and had different civil organizations who supported or initiated them, thus they required different design and evaluation frameworks and as a result had different e-Tool needs.

After discussions with municipal leaders the following was concluded. There was strong will to reach a large constituency face-to-face (as that was the factor that brought them the election results). They need tools that have a high chance to be successfully applied in increasing activity of residents. But there is a risk associated with complex tools: (their use, management, time to implement and test), versus existing tools with limited scope and functionality but readily usable and known to the public. On the other hand it would be hard to later transfer to an integrated platform. Technology should help in limiting the influence of negative contextual factors (such as anger, trolls, and deep political divide) - without being politically or administratively too restrictive. Staff had a limited ePart IT knowledge and the offices had limited financial resources. Even running existing systems and updating the website strained IT operations personnel. Overall, they need to use a mix of technology and other methods, as building connections was more important than using technology.

7   Options: Evaluation of Tools Considered

As a starting point the municipality had a (registration-based) email distribution list, a website, and a Facebook page. The questions were how to utilize these in the future and whether the district should operate its own participatory platform. Due to financial, technical and personnel restrictions it was not an option to design and develop a new ePart platform. However, they could install and run a freeware solution, while there was also discussion about the opportunity to collaborate with other districts to share one. Ultimately, they could wait for the technology platform contemplated by the city level municipality (and utilize that once available). The municipal website was under redesign, with first offering static capabilities (but being more informative, and regularly updated with fresh news) and later potentially being augmented with 2.0 features.

There were issues with social media integration. There was a clear need to foster community and there indeed was a municipal Facebook (FB) page with small but active group of participants. But the future role of Facebook as a readily available communication channel was not straightforward. Although FB definitely falls short of a deliberative platform the options were: a) do not use; b) use only for dissemination; c) use for basic group discussions or d) rely more on it through forums, votes, and community building. While FB is global and widely used, the question remains whether it would be beneficial (or even possible) to build a new, local social media solution. They could perhaps utilize Twitter for offering fast access to interesting bits of up-to-date information and collecting issues. Furthermore, the applicability of social media tools in deliberation is questionable (in general). On the other hand, social interaction has benefits for partici-patory engagement in general - and is encouraged by municipal leaders. Besides, local authorities wanted to take advantage of the existing civil group on FB. However, if FB is used for such goal then data would be controlled by a third party and integration with a (potential future) local deliberative platform might become difficult (beyond linking from the platform to Facebook and other SM sites). Table 1 presents an overview of evaluating the technology options considered by the municipality.

Table 1. Overview of tool options

Tool	Main functionality(s)	Reach	Complexity	Costs
Deliberative platform	Form assemblies, run projects, deliberation	Younger, active residents	Running: medium managing: high	High
Shared platform	Form assemblies, run projects, deliberation	Younger, active residents	Running: medium	Shared (medium)
Discussion forum (2.0) on website	Idea generation; moderated discussion and sharing opinion	Need to be advertised	Low	Medium-low
Web site	Disseminating information; sharing project ideas	Those already online	Medium	Medium
Email list	Disseminating information	Older generation	Low	Low
General social media	Disseminating information; raising opinions; non-moderated discussion	Those already online - age dependent	Low	Low

If they delay the decision on a platform, but release the new website, there are pressing questions to face: a) what features the website should have and b) how a later deploy-ment of a platform would be influenced by the website (if successful) or a strengthened Facebook presence. IT-based tools and techniques thus could be a useful addition to the repertoire, but with the current goals of reaching out and perceived extra work to be done, district authorities did not make it a priority. Furthermore, given the complexity of running their own platform (as an alternative to the popular social media riddled with disadvantages or augmenting the existing web sites with 2.0 capabilities), districts decided to wait if there is a platform offered at the capital level they could utilize.

8 Discussion: Status of Critical Success Factors

This Section reviews the CSFs (and related barriers) as summarized in Sect. 5. One of the key political factors is "Commitment by the government". Indeed, the new district major had acted fast. The first step towards participatory involvement – just a few weeks after the election – was the appointment of a "participation" consultant with the job to set the direction and who had a (small) budget to assemble a part-time team.

Following our recommendation, the municipal "Participation" team first considered potential issues and identified the following main barriers. Most importantly, there was no substantial history of civil participation in the works of the municipality – not only online, but in general: apart from a few active individuals and a handful of civil organizations resident engagement had to be built up from scratch. This has made it even more difficult to engage in an ePart program. Also – and consequently – there were no accepted norms and ways how to get civil players involved and how to collaborate with them successfully. There was no routine at either side, and it was not in the thinking of citizens. In addition, even after the first meetings there was clear resistance on the side of administration. Not only new policies and internal rules were required but there appeared to be a clear need for a culture change and related education.

The previous Section has reviewed the external factors related to technology and thus covered the corresponding CSF as concluded from the literature (i.e. Usability of tools). It was recognized that the key to success is building relationships quickly, relying on existing connections and basic communication channels. They organized town-hall meetings advertised through old-fashioned ways of using public displays as well as through FB and by sending out emails to existing receiver lists. Although it was more out of necessity, it still fits the requirement of combining online with offline channels for communication. Again, the desire to act fast – and thus take advantage of the political momentum of winning the election from the position of being in opposition – had resulted in a situation when there was no "[t]horough communication and promotion plan" ready yet.

Regarding security and privacy it was a tough choice between anonymous posting that allows privacy and using names for credibility. It was decided, that – irrespective the actual technological solution to be selected – participation in certain discussions should definitely require proof of local residence (and this capability was enlisted as an important requirement).

To address organizational issues the major initiated the revision of all internal policies dealing with resident services. Although this is not directly related to participation, this was decided to the first step in changing the culture – and to see individual reactions. No training of sensitivity have been initiated yet. Interestingly, why there was a participation project initiated and a participation officer role established whose task was to set the strategy and organize training, there was no participation policy created.

As mentioned in Sect. 2 there were several ongoing projects which had already gathered (albeit limited) civil attention. The decision was made to built on these ongoing cases to expand reach. As suitable technology was not yet available, exhibitions and face-to-face meetings were organized where the municipality invited not only local residents but representatives of the city level and experts from the architect teams who were involved in the revitalization projects. These meetings were quite successful and allowed the participatory team to collect online data. Meetings were video recorded and made available to further advertise the cause and to show they take their promise seriously. Strictly speaking however, these open, general meetings do not provide the best way of handling the complexity inherent in many of the topics addressed. Quality of participation is hard to judge as there were question-answer sections, but no small-group discussion or voting took place, neither there were any actual decisions made at any of the meetings. However, the participatory advisor had a novel idea of collecting ideas using an offline method of a display: at the local market a large poster was installed with the map of a street to be revitalized and passersby could use post its to add recommendations, ideas or suggestions to the map (see Fig. 1).

Fig. 1. Offline idea collection for the revitalization of a local street (photo by Author)

Regarding future projects a process management framework has been put together (based on literature case study recommendations) – but it has not been used yet. Based on best practice advice, beyond the current ongoing projects the rules for new initiatives recommend planning with generous timescales; establishing clear project boundaries and goals (as much as possible – but with flexibility), focused definition of tasks, preparation of participants (e.g. providing ample information through a diverse selection of channels). Also, for online discussions the use of a facilitator is considered – although at the current time there are no trained people available locally. Internal communication has to be improved. Projects that get a go ahead need to come with contingency plans.

9   Conclusions, Limitations and Future Research

In the case presented contextual readiness seemed, as predicted by literature, just as important as technology itself. Indeed, while there are reasonable options to step on the "electronic" avenue of participation, the local authority had not only limited resources and expertise, their priority under the given political-social circumstances was to meet people directly. The main, stated goal was to rebuild trust in local political leadership. The use of technology took a back seat, at least for now. Furthermore, considering the efforts required to install, run, and manage a full-blown participation platform, it should be done when critical mass is reachable, may be through sharing the work with other district municipalities. This path of introducing ICT was further reinforced by the expected cost relative to the limited budget available. Beyond the lack of trust another disadvantage of moving towards ePart is the expected complexity (and lack of expertise) of combining off- and online solutions. A gradual shift would also allow time for municipal leaders to experiment with incentives offered to citizens or motivators that could help shift culture from face-to-face to online, or at least mixed participation.

The research reported has only covered one municipality for a few months. More information collection is needed about the exact nature of local context especially in relation to the anecdotal "apathy" (no reliable scientific source investigating the issue have been located dealing with the attitude of residents in the capital or its districts). This research is planned to be continued for several more years and the intention is to monitor both the offline and online progress of the participatory initiative and a deeper understanding of the motivation of the various stakeholders is a priority along with an analysis of tool use. In addition, there are four more districts, who appear to be on the same track and face the same questions: contact has been made with them too, and successful collaboration could help shad even more light on what a new ePart initiative may encounter especially in a difficult political context.

References

1. Baguma, J.: Is there hope in ICTs for Africa? Developing an e-Participation model to improve the status of public service delivery in Uganda. In: Conference for E-Democracy and Open Government, pp. 225–238. Donau-Universität, Krems (2015)
2. Bohman, J.: Survey article: the coming of age of deliberative democracy. J. Polit. Philos. 6(4), 400–425 (1998)
3. Booher, D.E.: Collaborative governance practices and democracy. Natl. Civ. Rev. 93(4), 32–46 (2004)
4. Chadwick, A.: Bringing e-democracy back in: why it matters for future research on e-governance. Soc. Sci. Comput. Rev. 21(4), 443–455 (2003)
5. Dahler-Larsen, P.: From programme theory to constructivism. On tragic, magic and competing programmes. Evaluation 7(3), 331–349 (2001)
6. Grönlund, Å.: Introduction to the special issue on e-democracy in practice: methods, infrastructures and discourse. E-Serv. J. 2(1), 3–8 (2002)
7. Held, A.: Models of Democracy. Blackwell Publishers, Cambridge (1996)
8. Hepburn, P.: Local democracy in a digital age: lessons for local government from the Manchester congestion charge referendum. Local Gov. Stud. 40(1), 82–101 (2014)
9. Islam, M.S.: Towards a sustainable e-Participation implementation model. Eur. J. ePractice 5(10), 1–12 (2008)
10. Kabanov, Y., Chugunov, A.V.: Electronic "pockets of effectiveness": E-governance and institutional change in St. Petersburg, Russia. In: Janssen, M., et al. (eds.) EGOV 2017. LNCS, vol. 10428, pp. 386–398. Springer, Cham (2017). https://doi.org/10.1007/978-3-319-64677-0_32
11. Kneuer, M., Harnisch, S.: Diffusion of e-government and e-participation in Democracies and Autocracies. Glob. Policy 7(4), 548–556 (2016)

12. Kubicek, H., Aichholzer, G.: Closing the evaluation gap in e-Participation research and practice. In: Aichholzer, G., Kubicek, H., Torres, L. (eds.) Evaluating e-Participation. PAIT, vol. 19, pp. 11–45. Springer, Cham (2016). https://doi.org/10.1007/978-3-319-25403-6_2

13. Loukis, E.: Evaluating eParticipation projects and lessons learnt. In: Charalabidis, Y., Koussouris, S. (eds.) Empowering Open and Collaborative Governance, pp. 95–115. Springer, Berlin (2012). https://doi.org/10.1007/978-3-642-27219-6_6

14. Macintosh, A.: Characterizing e-Participation in policy-making. In: Proceedings of the 37th Annual Hawaii International Conference on System Sciences, p. 10 (2004)

15. Macintosh, A., Whyte, A.: Towards an evaluation framework for eParticipation. Transform. Gov. People Process Policy 2(1), 16–30 (2008)

16. Norris, D.F., Reddick, C.G.: E-democracy at the American grassroots: not now… not likely? Inf. Polity 18(3), 201–216 (2013)

17. OECD: Promise and Problems of E-Democracy: Challenges of Online Citizen Engagement. OECD, Paris (2003). https://www.oecd.org/gov/digital-government/35176328.pdf

18. Panopoulou, E., Tambouris, E., Tarabanis, K.: eParticipation initiatives in Europe: learning from practitioners. In: Tambouris, E., Macintosh, A., Glassey, O. (eds.) ePart 2010. LNCS, vol. 6229, pp. 54–65. Springer, Heidelberg (2010). https://doi.org/10.1007/978-3-642-151 58-3_5

19. Panopoulou, E., Tambouris, E., Tarabanis, K.: Success factors in designing eParticipation initiatives. Inf. Organ. 24(4), 195–213 (2014)

20. Parycek, P., Sachs, M., Sedy, F., Schossböck, J.: Evaluation of an E-participation project: lessons learned and success factors from a cross-cultural perspective. In: Tambouris, E., Macintosh, A., Bannister, F. (eds.) ePart 2014. LNCS, vol. 8654, pp. 128–140. Springer, Heidelberg (2014). https://doi.org/10.1007/978-3-662-44914-1_11

21. Pflughoeft, B.R., Schneider, I.E.: Social media as E-participation: can a multiple hierarchy stratification perspective predict public interest? Gov. Inf. Q. 37(1), 101422 (2020)

22. Pratchett, L.: Local autonomy, local democracy and the 'new localism'. Polit. Stud. 52(2), 358–375 (2004)

23. Primus, N., Effing, R., Groot, B., Veenstra, M., de Vries, S.: Innovative public participation in the twenty-first century. In: EGOV-CeDEM-EPart 2018, pp. 101–114. Donau-Universität, Krems (2018)

24. Santamaría-Philco, A., Cerdá, J.H.C., Gramaje, M.C.P.: Advances in e-Participation: a perspective of Last Years. IEEE Access 7, 155894–155916 (2019)

25. Scherer, S., Wimmer, M.A.: Reference framework for E-participation projects. In: Tambouris, E., Macintosh, A., de Bruijn, H. (eds.) ePart 2011. LNCS, vol. 6847, pp. 145–156. Springer, Heidelberg (2011). https://doi.org/10.1007/978-3-642-23333-3_13

26. Smith, S., Macintosh, A., Millard, J.: A three-layered framework for evaluating e-participation. Int. J. Electron. Gov. 4(4), 304–321 (2011)

27. Steinbach, M., Süß, S.: Administrators' identities and strategies in the e-participation innovation process. Inf. Polity 23(3), 281–305 (2018)

28. Wakabi, W., Grönlund, Å.: When SNS use doesn't trigger e-Participation: case study of an African Authoritarian Regime. In: Civic Engagement and Politics, pp. 1125–1142. IGI Global (2019)

Trust in Citizens and Forms of Political Participation: The View of Public Managers

Joachim Åström$^{(\boxtimes)}$ (iD) and Martin Karlsson (iD)

Örebro University, 70182 Örebro, Sweden
{Joachim.astrom,Martin.karlsson}@oru.se

Abstract. Like all forms of collaborative governance, new forms of citizen participation include risk-taking and therefore depend on mutual trust between the collaborating actors. While there is a huge body of research on citizens' trust in governments, public officials' trust in citizens has received very little scholarly attention. In order to address this gap, this paper draws on a recent survey of a representative sample of public managers in local Swedish government (N = 1430). Do public managers think that citizens are trustworthy? Does trust in citizens impact which forms of citizen participation public managers prefer? Even though public officials are more trusting than the general populous, we show that not every public official do trust citizens. Furthermore, the results show public managers' trust in citizens influences their attitudes towards new forms of participation. Just as citizens' political trust has a positive impact on some forms of participation, but not on others, managers' trust in citizens matters more for some forms of participation than others.

Keywords: Citizen participation · E-participation · Public officials · Public managers · Trust

1 Introduction

With the aim of increasing trust in government, new forms of citizen participation are coming into play in local politics. Democratic innovations [1, 20], co-production of services [2], and participatory planning [3] are all common approaches for promoting direct citizen participation in policymaking. In recent years, e-participation tools have significantly improved the methodological quality of these initiatives, which has made their supporters believe that e-participation will renew democracy, offer a remedy for political populism, and enhance trust in government.

While some barriers to a more participatory democracy certainly have been removed through technical advancements, others are more lasting. One such enduring barrier is the attitude of public officials [4, 5]. Even if public officials tend to be in favor of the idea of e-participation, they do not always support e-participation in practice. The gap between policy talk and action is debated today [21] as much as it was in the 1960s [12]. Our understanding of the gap between theory and practice is nevertheless far from

S. Hofmann et al. (Eds.): ePart 2020, LNCS 12220, pp. 15–25, 2020.
https://doi.org/10.1007/978-3-030-58141-1_2

complete. In this article we argue that new forms of participation, like all forms of collaborative governance, include risk-taking and therefore depend on the existence of mutual trust between the collaborating actors. Previous research has done a great job of investigating trust from the standpoint of citizens' trust in government. However, there is almost no research on what public officials think about their relationship with the public, the extent to which they trust citizens, or why they do or do not trust citizens [6, 7]. If it is true that "trust begets trust, while distrust begets distrust," this is a significant research gap.

When it comes to citizens, we know that political trust has a positive impact on some forms of participation, but not on others. Previous research has shown that distrusting citizens are more likely to engage in non-institutionalized forms of political participation, which are often goal-oriented, issue-specific and situated outside the institutions of the political system. On the other hand, citizens with high levels of political trust are more likely to engage in institutionalized forms of political participation. Public managers' trust in citizens impacts their willingness to invite citizens to participate in various forms of government/democratic processes has yet to be examined. In this context, the aim of this article is to expand our understanding of public managers' trust in citizens in relation to two research questions: (1) Do public managers think that citizens are trustworthy? (2) Does public managers' trust in citizens have an impact of which forms of participation public managers prefer?

We will use a survey that targeted a representative sample of public managers in local government in Sweden (N = 1430). The first section presents the theoretical framework, which ends with some hypotheses related to public managers' trust in citizens. After having reviewed the literature and presented the data, this article proceeds with the empirical analysis of the hypotheses, followed by a concluding discussion of its findings and their implications.

2 Theory

One claim in the literature about citizens' participation is that participation requires political trust. Almond and Verba [8, p. 27] establish that in order to become a participant in politics, citizens require a positive opinion of the political system. Negative attitudes towards or negative judgements of the political system lead to alienation that erodes the effectiveness and legitimacy of the democratic system and will lead to democratic instability over time [8, p. 22 & 230]. Another claim has been that distrust can serve a motivating factor for political participation. When political decision makers or the political system as a whole are perceived to be untrustworthy, citizens feel compelled to intervene [9]. More recent research shows that political trust has a positive impact on conventional forms of participation, but not on unconventional [10].

When it comes to public officials, trust in citizens is required in order to make participation meaningful. As Reed [11] argues, trust and control are opposing options for handling risk and can be viewed as two sides of the same analytic coin. Accordingly, we would expect public managers with little trust in their citizens to take more control over decision-making processes in order to make themselves less vulnerable to citizens. There are plenty of examples of this in the literature [22]. For instance, it is commonly believed that politically controversial topics should be avoided, while citizens are invited to participate in non-conflictual and non-political issues instead. Another familiar pattern is that citizen participation processes are disconnected from formal decision-making processes and that the lack of a facilitating institutional landscape impedes any policy impact. Interpreted under Arnstein's [12] prominent eight-rung ladder of participation, many of these initiatives are labeled as tokenistic.

While empirical research shows that public officials support the idea of citizen participation, it also indicates that their orientations regarding citizen participation in practice are less attuned to abstract normative goals than to concerns with concrete instrumental costs and benefits [4, 5, 13]. Potential benefits include making the work of government more acceptable to citizens and making decision-making more effective. Potential risks and uncertainties are associated with time, money, and other resources. Additionally, citizen participation may exacerbate conflicts or result in the undue influence of uninformed individuals and therefore become ineffective [14]. The implementation of participation implies that lower degrees of trust in citizens may lead to reduced risk-taking, less involvement and more control of citizens. In contrast, higher degrees of trust should be expected to increase risk-taking and motivate steps up 'the ladder of participation' [12].

In order to examine how trusting citizens relates to preferred forms of participation, we will include a stepwise approach including the advantages and disadvantages of participation.

3 Data and Measurements

3.1 Data

Public managers are largely responsible for designing, implementing, and making use of the results of participatory processes. Hence, they largely determine the outcome of government initiated participatory processes [4, 5]. In Swedish local government, there are about 31,000 public managers. In order to examine their attitudes towards citizens, a random sample of 3,000 individuals—registered as managers and employed by a Swedish local government—was generate using the occupational register. Statistics Sweden curated the sample and facilitated the data collection by way of a broad survey in 2018. The survey included questions and statements related to twenty-five topics of which one measured public officials' perceived trust in citizens. The total number of responses to the survey reached 1,430, a 48% response rate.

Out of the 1,430 city managers in the data set, 32% are men and 68% are women, which illustrates the major changes that have taken place during recent decades when it comes to leadership and gender in Swedish local government. Not long ago, these numbers would have been reversed. About half of the respondents were 55 years of age or older, and the non-response analysis revealed an underrepresentation of managers under the age of 35 (response rate of 24%).

Table 1. Operationalizations and measurements.

Concept	Operationalization	Variable	Scale
Trust in citizens	Assesses how the respondents perceive citizens' integrity, knowledge, and benevolence	Additive Index based on six items. Scale ranging from 0 (strongly disagree) to 3 (strongly agree)	0–18 α: 0.748
Referenda	Measures the extent to which respondents think that local government should extend the use of referenda	Single item. Scale ranging from 0 (do not agree) to 4 (strongly agree)	0–4
Initiative	Measures the extent to which respondents think that local government should expand citizen initiatives	Single item. Scale ranging from 0 (do not agree) to 4 (strongly agree)	0–4
Citizen dialogues	Measures the extent to which respondents think that local government should expand citizen dialogues	Single item. Scale ranging from 0 (do not agree) to 4 (strongly agree)	0–4
Advantages of participation	Assesses the respondents' view of advantages of citizen participation	Index variable based on four items. Scale ranging from 0 (do not agree) to 3 (strongly agree)	0–12 α: 0.842
Disadvantages of participation	Assesses the respondents' view of disadvantages of citizen participation	Index variable based on three items. Scale ranging from 0 (do not agree) to 3 (strongly agree)	0–9 α: 0.602

3.2 Measurements

Regardless of the underlying perspective (micro or macro), being confident that one's expectations of another will be fulfilled and a willingness to be vulnerable are critical components of most definitions of trust. In the definition given by Rousseau et al. [15, p. 395], "trust is a psychological state comprising the intention to accept vulnerability based upon positive expectations of another". As informed by Yang [6] and Vigoda-Gadot [16], we further understand trust to be reflected in three dimensions: the perception of competence, benevolence, and integrity. Competence refers to citizens' ability to act on their intentions. Benevolence and integrity address the intentions of the trustee, with benevolence being the intention to act 'in a kind way' toward the trustor and integrity being the underlying moral principles guiding behavior.

The main independent variable was measured via six items, which were assessed with the following questions: "Citizens I interact with through my profession are generally… (1) reliable," (2) "sincere and honest in their interactions with the local government," (3) "well aware of local government affairs and current issues," (4) "knowledgeable of how the local government organization works," (5) "committed to changing and improving the municipality," and (6) "more concerned about what benefits the municipality as a whole than what benefits them personally," The Likert-type scale ranged from 0 (strongly disagree) to 3 (strongly agree). The Cronbach's alpha was 0.748, demonstrating good reliability of this measure as an independent variable.

Perceived advantages of participation were measured through four survey items each measured on a Likert-type scale ranging from 0 (strongly disagree) to 3 (strongly agree). Managers were asked to what extent they agreed with the following statements: "Citizen participation in local politics will lead to" (1) "better policy decisions," (2) "more political equality," (3) "more satisfied citizens," and (4) "more trust in the local government among citizens." The four items were combined to an additive index measuring perceived advantages of citizen participation. Similarly, perceived disadvantages of citizen participation were measured with three items on an identical 0–3 scale. Managers were asked to agree or disagree with the following statements: "Citizen participation in local politics will lead to" (1) "worse policy decisions," (2) "greater political inequality," and (3) "more conflicts in the community." These items were combined to an additive index measuring managers' perceptions of disadvantages of citizen participation.

Finally, the main dependent variables were measured via three variables, measuring the managers' attitudes towards an extended use of (1) citizen initiatives, (2) referenda, and (3) citizen dialogues. The Likert-type scale ranged from 0 (strongly disagree) to 4 (strongly agree). All the measurements used are summarized in Table 1 above.

4 Empirical Results

4.1 Public Managers Trust in Citizens

Previous research has indicated that while most public officials support citizen participation in theory, they remain skeptical about the concrete instrumental costs and benefits of citizen participation [5, 13]. Engaging citizens in political participation may have the potential benefits of increasing citizens' acceptance of the government and generating more effective decision-making. However, there are also potential risks and uncertainties associated with citizen participation as it may increase the workload of public administration and place an added financial burden on public institutions. Implementing processes for citizen participation requires an allocation of public resources that could be used in other capacities. There is also a possibility that citizen participation could lead to more conflict or become ineffective as uninformed citizens gain influence on public policy.

This implies that a low degree of trust in citizens may lead public managers to avoid the risk-taking associated with citizen participation, fostering fewer advantages of citizen involvement and ultimately less public control over policy-making. In contrast, a high level of government trust in citizens can foster a greater willingness for public managers to accept the risk allowing citizen participation and motivate them to support such practices further up on 'the ladder of participation' [12].

To further understand the factors influencing public managers' support for citizen participation we therefore find it vital to analyze public managers' level of trust in citizens. Do managers trust citizens? And to what extent? In Table 2 below, we present analyses of public managers' trust in citizens when it comes to citizens' integrity, ability, and benevolence. Public managers report positive evaluations of citizens' integrity, perceiving citizens to be reliable, sincere, and honest in their interactions with local government. Around 80% of managers agree that citizens have integrity. Managers' perceptions of citizens' ability and benevolence were less positive. Only a minority agreed that citizens are aware of local government affairs and current issues, and fewer than 1 in 4 agreed that citizens are knowledgeable about how the local government organization works. Turning to benevolence, 45% of the managers agree that citizens are committed to change and improve the municipality, but only 16% percent believe that citizens are more concerned with what benefits the municipality as a whole than with what benefits them personally.

Table 2. Public managers' trust in citizens (Given in percentage that agree with the survey items)

Citizens I interact with in my work are generally. . .	
1. Reliable	83%
2. Sincere and honest in their interactions with local government	79%
3. Aware of local government affairs and current issues	39%
4. Knowledgeable about how the local government organization works	21%
5. Committed to changing and improving the municipality	45%
6. More concerned about what benefits the municipality as a whole than what benefits them personally	16%
Trust in citizens index (high)	48%

Comment: N = 1359–1381; Scales range between 0 (strongly disagree) to 3 (strongly agree).

4.2   Trust and the Advantages and Disadvantages of Citizen Participation

Does public managers' trust in citizens influence their attitudes towards citizen participation in politics? Although previous research on this subject is scarce, a study among public administrators in the US suggests a connection between trust and a favorable opinion of citizen participation [14]. We investigated this relationship by way of bivariate correlation analyses between the index of public managers' trust in citizens (described above) and managers' perceptions of potential advantages and disadvantages of citizen participation in politics.

Starting with perceived advantages of citizen participation (see Table 3 below), we find positive and statistically significant correlations across all items. Public managers with greater trust in citizens are more prone to believe that citizen participation leads to better policy decisions, greater political equality, more satisfied citizens and increased trust in the local government among citizens. Furthermore, we find a positive and statistically significant correlation between an additive index of all items measuring advantages of participation and managers' trust in citizens.

Table 3. Association between public managers' trust in citizens and perceived advantages of citizen participation

	Pearson correlation	Sig.	N
Better decisions	0.172	0.000	1322
Greater political equality	0.141	0.000	1309
More satisfied citizens	0.191	0.000	1314
Greater trust in the local government	0.174	0.000	1320
Index	0.210	0.000	1289

However, managers' trust in citizens does not positively correlate with perceived disadvantage of citizen participation (see Table 4 below). Public managers with weaker trust in citizens are not more disposed to believe that citizen participation risks impediments to the quality of decision making, the degree of political equality or decreased conflict in society. Hence, the perceived risks of citizen participation are not connected to the level of managers' trust in citizens. Potentially such perceptions of disadvantages might be connected to normative views of democracy. For instance, proponents of electoral democracy have often argued that extensive citizen participation outside of elections will lead to decreased political equality [19].

Table 4. Association between public managers' trust in citizens and perceived disadvantages of citizen participation

	Pearson correlation	Sig.	N
Worse decisions	−0.038	0.174	1314
Greater political inequality	−0.043	0.122	1314
More conflicts in society	−0.012	0.657	1309
Index	−0.042	0.134	1299

4.3   Trust and Attitudes Towards Different Forms of Participation

Thus far we have established that public managers' trust in citizens is associated with citizen participation as it influences managers' perceptions of the advantages of citizens' political participation. Public managers act as potential gatekeepers in relation to the processes of citizen participation with decisive influence over whether and how participatory processes are implemented. Therefore, it is important to learn more about how managers' trust in citizens directly shapes their attitudes towards different forms of citizen participation. Are managers who trust citizens more prone to support citizens' participation in politics? And does the influence of trust vary across different forms of participation, as it does among citizens [10]?

In Table 5 (below), bivariate correlation analyses are presented, investigating the association among trust, perceived advantages and disadvantages of citizen participation and public managers' support for three forms of citizen participation. These forms of participation are citizen dialogues, citizens' right to advocate for issues with the local council, and local referenda. We find positive and statistically significant associations between trust in citizens and support for citizen dialogues as well as for referenda. However, we find no significant association between trust and initiatives.

Table 5. Association between trust in citizens and the perceived advantages and disadvantages of citizens' participation and attitudes towards

	Citizen dialogues	Initiatives	Referenda
Trust in citizens	0.110^{***}	0.017	0.07^{*}
Advantages of participation–Index	0.430^{***}	0.205^{***}	0.131^{***}
Disadvantages of participation–Index	-0.254^{***}	-0.084^{**}	-0.059^{*}
N	1330–1349	1330–1349	1325–1342

Statistical significance displayed as follows: ***: $p<.001$; **: $p<.01$; *: $p<.05$

Perceived advantages of participation are strongly associated with support for citizen dialogues and positively correlated with support for initiatives and referenda. Perceived disadvantages of participation is negatively associated with support for all three forms of citizen participation. The strongest negative association is between perceived disadvantages and support for citizen dialogues. This result might be surprising since referenda form a much more influential and disruptive form of citizen participation. However, the strong associations between the perceived advantages and disadvantage of participation and support for citizen dialogues may well stem from the fact that Swedish public managers have a stronger gatekeeper function in relation to citizen dialogues as compared to the other two forms of participation investigated.

Taking the analysis one step further, we consider the potential indirect effect of public managers' trust in citizens on their support of citizen participation. As demonstrated above, trust influences managers' perceptions of the advantages of participation, which in turn influences their support for participation. Hence, in addition to the direct association between trust and the level of support for citizen dialogues and referenda discussed above, it is also clear that managers' trust influences support for participation indirectly—by way of influencing managers' perceptions of the advantages of participation. The direct and indirect associations between managers' trust and their support for different forms of participation are summarized in Fig. 1 below.

This mediation or path-analysis allows us to better grasp the full scope of the importance of managers' trust in citizens regarding the process of citizen participation. The

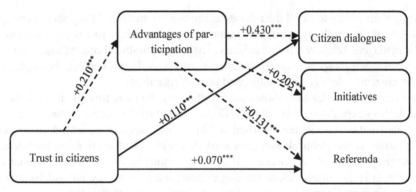

Fig. 1. Direct and indirect influence of public managers' trust in citizens on their support for different forms of participation.

direct, indirect, and total effects of managers' trust in citizens on their support for different forms of citizen participation are described in Table 6 below. The indirect effect is calculated as the product of the association between trust and the perceived advantages and the association between the perceived advantages and political managers' support for the respective forms of participation. The total effect is calculated as the sum of the direct and indirect effects. Only statistically significant associations ($p < 0.05$) are included in these calculations.

Table 6. Direct, indirect, and total effects of political managers' trust in citizens on their support for political participation.

	Citizen dialogues	Initiatives	Referenda
Direct effect	0.110	–	0.070
Indirect effect	$(0.210 \times 0.430) = 0.090$	–	$(0.210 \times 0.131) = 0.028$
Total effect	0.200	–	0.098

The analyses presented in Table 6 show that trust in citizens is of non-trivial importance for understanding public managers' attitudes towards citizen participation in politics. Managers who trust citizens more are disposed towards supporting citizen dialogues as well as referenda as compared to less trusting managers. Hence, building trust between citizens and public managers might be a pivotal step for supporting e-participation processes, as has been suggested in case studies [17].

5   Conclusions

As Newman et al. [18] reminds us, new forms of participation do not displace old forms of governance; rather, they interact with each other. This creates opposing imperatives for public managers. They should encourage participation from their citizens while ensuring their ability to fulfill their duties as imposed from above. They should engage in long-term trust building, while also competently completing tasks in the short term. Public managers' relationship with citizens exist in an institutional context where citizen participation has its specific costs, advantages, and risks. In this context, the degree of trust in citizens' integrity, knowledge, and benevolence matters.

While earlier studies have shown public officials to be more trusting than people in general, this study shows many public officials do not trust citizens. Furthermore, we have found that trust in citizens is related to the perceived advantages and risks of citizen participation. If the political managers trust their citizens, there is more confidence in potential benefits of participation. If there is distrust in the citizens, the value of participation is questioned. Thus, trusting citizens seems to be key for understanding whether or not public managers think that participation is worth the effort.

Furthermore, the results show that trusting citizens influences public managers' attitudes towards new forms of participation. Just like citizens' political trust has a positive impact on some forms of participation, but not on others, managers' trust in citizens matters more for some forms of participation than others. Somewhat surprisingly, citizen dialogues show the greatest impact from perceived advantages, risks and trust in citizens. At first glance at least, this seems contradictory to the idea that trust and control are opposing forces for handling risk. Regarding referenda, more control over decisions is given to citizens than in dialogues. However, the normative view of direct democracy versus representative democracy is more important in relation to referenda. One potential explanation for the pattern is that normative issues are less salient in relation to dialogues, which makes instrumental factors more important in shaping managers' attitudes towards participation.

The literature on new forms of participation predominately considers the drivers and barriers towards e-participation in normative terms while recognizing the role of public managers in facilitating change [4, 5]. Our examination indicates that we should make more effort to understand how the perceptions of the instrumental costs, benefits and risks associated with citizens' political participation is affected by public officials' trust in citizens. Knowledge about public officials' trust in citizens could have important policy implications. If we know what institutional arrangements influence public officials' trust in citizens, it might be possible to address these factors through policy measures. New forms of participation provide a great opportunity for experimenting with trust-building arrangements; however, past research and development activities have typically had a one-sided focus, trying to find mechanisms that close the political distance between citizens and governments. This study reveals that we also need to aim for institutional arrangements that increase public managers' trust in citizens.

References

1. Smith, G.: Democratic Innovations: Designing Institutions for Citizen Participation. Cambridge University Press, Cambridge (2009)
2. Alford, J.: Engaging Public Sector Clients: From Service-Delivery to Co-Production. Palgrave Macmillan, New York (2009)
3. Innes, J.E., Booher, D.E.: Reframing public participation: strategies for the 21st century. Plan. Theory Pract. 5(4), 419–436 (2004)

4. Moynihan, D.P.: Normative and instrumental perspectives on public participation. Am. Rev. Public Adm. **32**(2), 164–188 (2003)
5. Liao, Y., Schachter, H.L.: Exploring the antecedents of municipal managers' attitudes towards citizen participation. Public Manag. Rev. **20**(9), 1287–1308 (2018)
6. Yang, K.: Public administrators' trust in citizens: a missing link in citizen involvement efforts. Public Adm. Rev. **65**(3), 273–285 (2005)
7. Moyson, S., Van de Walle, S., Groeneveld, S.: What do public officials think about citizens? The role of public officials' trust and their perceptions of citizens' trustworthiness in interactive governance. In: Edelenbos, J., Van Meerkerk, I. (eds.) Critical reflections on interactive governance. Self-Organization and Participation in Public Governance, pp. 189–208. Edward Elgar, Cheltenham (2016)
8. Verba, S., Almond, G.: The Civic Culture: Political Attitudes and Democracy in Five Nations. Princeton University Press, Princeton (1963)
9. Barnes, S.H., Kaase, M.: Political Action: Mass Participation in Five Western Democracies. SAGE, New York (1979)
10. Hooghe, M., Marien, S.: A comparative analysis of the relation between political trust and forms of political participation in Europe. Eur. Soc. **15**(1), 131–152 (2013)
11. Reed, M.I.: Organization, trust, and control: a realist analysis. Organ. Stud. **22**(2), 201–228 (2001)
12. Arnstein, S.: A ladder of citizen participation. J. Am. Inst. Plan. **35**(4), 216–224 (1969)
13. Åström, J., Granberg, M.: Urban planners, wired for change? Understanding elite support for e-participation. J. Inf. Technol. Polit. **4**(2), 63–77 (2007)
14. Yang, K., Callahan, K.: Citizen involvement efforts and bureaucratic responsiveness: participatory values, stakeholder pressures, and administrative practicality. Public Adm. Rev. **67**(2), 249–264 (2007)
15. Rousseau, D.M., Sitkin, S.B., Burt, R.S., Camerer, C.: Not so different after all: a cross-discipline view of trust. Acad. Manag. Rev. **23**(3), 393–404 (1998)
16. Vigoda-Gadot, E., Zalmanovitch, Y., Belonogov, A.: Public servants' trust in citizens: an extension of theory and an empirical examination with structural equation modeling (SEM). Public Organ. Rev. **12**(4), 383–399 (2012)
17. Adenskog, M., Åström, J., Ertiö, T., Karlsson, M., Ruoppila, S., Thiel, S.-K.: Balancing potential and risk: the living lab approach in mobile participation research. In: Parycek, P., et al. (eds.) ePart 2017. LNCS, vol. 10429, pp. 12–23. Springer, Cham (2017). https://doi.org/10.1007/978-3-319-64322-9_2
18. Newman, J., Barnes, M., Sullivan, H., Knops, A.: Public participation and collaborative governance. J. Soc. Policy **33**(2), 203–223 (2004)
19. Gilljam, M., Hermansson, J.: Demokratins Mekanismer. Malmö, Liber (2003)
20. Åström, J., Jonsson, M.E., Karlsson, M.: Democratic innovations: reinforcing or changing perceptions of trust? Int. J. Public Adm. **40**(7), 575–587 (2017)
21. Åström, J.: Participatory urban planning: what would make planners trust the citizens? Urban Plan. (2020, forthcoming)
22. Åström, J.: Citizen participation. In: Orum, A.M. (ed.) The Wiley-Blackwell Encyclopedia of Urban and Regional Studies. Wiley-Blackwell, Malden (2019)

Digital Transformation

Investigation of Interoperability Governance: The Case of a Court Information System

Epameinondas Troulinos[1]([⊠]) and Efthimios Tambouris[2]

[1] Administrative Court of First Instance at Serres, K. Karamanli 53, Serres, Greece
etroulinos@adjustice.gr
[2] University of Macedonia, Egnatia 156, Thessaloniki, Greece
tambouris@uom.gr

Abstract. The latest version of European Union's European Interoperability Framework (EIF 2017) introduced the concept of 'interoperability governance' as a key enabler of interoperability. The paper examines this concept in an information system for the judiciary. It particularly explores how the governance structure of the Integrated Administrative Court Case Management System of Greece affected the decisions regarding interoperability. We use a case study methodology to achieve this goal. Our findings are consistent, in most parts, with the conceptual model of EIF 2017. We affirm that the requirement of independence of the judiciary imposes certain limits that have to be respected in an interoperability governance structure of the courts. We emphasize on the importance of dealing with certain issues of interoperability before the introduction of an information system in the judiciary. We conclude that a 'dynamic' governance structure, that is a structure that changes during the life cycle of an information system, is consistent with real world challenges that arise regarding interoperability.

Keywords: Interoperability · Interoperability governance · Administrative justice

1 Introduction

Several countries introduced ICT in their justice systems in order to improve both the efficiency of justice and accessibility to justice. For digital technology to be efficient for justice, it is necessary to encourage the secure flow of data between various IS; i.e. the data should circulate and be used easily. Different IS, both within and outside the judiciary, need to be made interoperable.

EU noticed the need for interoperable IS so as to deliver integrated public services to EU citizens. It regards interoperability "a key factor in making a digital transformation possible" since it "allows administrative entities to electronically exchange, amongst themselves and with citizens and businesses, meaningful information in ways that are understood by all parties" [1]. Furthermore, the latest version of the European Interoperability Framework (henceforth, EIF 2017) recognizes 'interoperability governance' as

© IFIP International Federation for Information Processing 2020
Published by Springer Nature Switzerland AG 2020
S. Hofmann et al. (Eds.): ePart 2020, LNCS 12220, pp. 29–40, 2020.
https://doi.org/10.1007/978-3-030-58141-1_3

a "the key to a holistic approach on interoperability, as it brings together all the instruments needed to apply it" and defines it as "decisions on interoperability frameworks, institutional arrangements, organizational structures, roles and responsibilities, policies, agreements and other aspects of ensuring and monitoring interoperability at national and EU levels" [1, Annex 2]. It further underlines the importance of political support and in-house skills to successfully implement interoperability policies and introduces a six-step-approach to manage standards and specifications.

Many public administrations were affected, as regards their system of organization, by the Weberian model and then shifted to the theoretical model of 'New Public Management' [2, with further citations]. The latter model was criticized [3] and the concept of 'governance' was introduced [2, with further citations] which "involves systematically determining, within a given scope, who makes each type of decision (decision rights), who provides input (input rights), and how people (or groups) will be held accountable for their role (accountability)" [4, with further citation].

Particularly in the judiciary, its governance structure is of extremely importance because it is related to the independence of courts; that is the need to guarantee judicial independence from the legislative and the executive branches of government. We assumed it is unlikely that a single form of governance will practically address all the issues regarding an IS for the judiciary. Since the judiciary does not usually have a specific governance structure for matters of interoperability or even for technology issues, the governance structure that it already has influences the governance structure that deals with interoperability issues. Therefore, it is crucial –from a governance point of view- to consider who is responsible for making the decisions that relate to interoperability (e.g. on technical and semantic standards, on necessary organizational and legal changes) and how it is ensured that they are adhered to. The aim of this paper is to examine the aforementioned issues in the governance structure of the Integrated Administrative Court Case Management System of Greece (henceforth, IACCMS); the IS that was introduced on 2015 in administrative justice of Greece. The relevant questions we wanted to explore were: 'what' were the main decisions regarding interoperability, 'who' had the mandate to make them and 'how' those decisions were implemented.

2   Related Work

Several works treat the problems of interoperability governance and governance of the judiciary.

On the issue of interoperability governance, [5–7] agreed that the central questions to be answered regarding 'governance' in IS are: 'what' are the main decisions, 'who' has the mandate to make them and 'how' those decisions are implemented. The 'who' question also addresses the issue of whether an existing actor or a new –permanent or temporary- actor will deal with those issues. Furthermore, the above mentioned authors agreed to three basic forms of governance for IS: a 'hierarchy', which refers to a central planning authority, a 'network', which refers to separate agencies that negotiate rules and a 'market', which refers to outsourcing of the operation of certain services. This observation is also consistent with institutional economic theory [8] as well as public management theory [9]. Other research, developed a definition of interoperability governance from a literature review and further developed a model template for inter-operability governance -which is similar to the Control OBjectives for Information and related Technology (COBIT) framework from the Information Systems Audit and Control Association (ISACA)- and tested it examining case studies in EU member states [10].

Several authors examined the concept of 'interoperability governance' and particularly the issue of the competent governing body. In a case study of a Swedish portal for business registration and management an argument was made in favor of a 'hierarchy' though in the concluding remarks it is stated that "in some cases, decentralization strengthens the integrity of the individual and autonomous actors, while in other cases it weakens actors by creating lock-in effects due to inflexible structures" [11]. However, in a case of the City of Munich overhaul of its ICT structures that focused on the dimension of governance, an argument was made in favor of a 'network' [12]. The same argument was supported on a presentation of the Danish approach to governance structures as regards the digital transformation of the public sector [13]. On the other hand, in a study of five cases of integrated electronic service delivery in Quebec, an argument was made in favor of a mixed governance structure [14]. The authors specifically introduced the concepts of 'vertical governance', i.e. "a management method that is hierarchically organized and structured according to formal rules laid down by the center" and 'horizontal governance', i.e. "a method of administration based on trust and collaboration among a network of organizations with no or little authority between them, with the aim of offering joint solutions to often complex problems" [14, with further citations]. The authors concluded that there are limits to horizontal governance structures and in order to overcome them they proposed the addition of vertical governance mechanisms, such as a central coordinating authority, that would be responsible for setting interoperability standards, modernizing administrative processes and providing a clear digital strategy.

Recently (January 2020), there was a proposal for a four step roadmap in order to develop a new integrated public service [15]. Regarding interoperability governance it stressed the importance of building political momentum and support (1st step, detect the need for change). It further indicated that the relevant governance structures should be set up during the next phase (2nd step, plan and select), without referring to any model of governance structure. Additionally, it suggested setting standards along with the overall framework (3rd stage, provide framework and set standards), then monitor the performance of the integrated service (4th stage, monitor and maintain) and, pursuant to the circumstances, begin the roadmap again.

On the issue of governance of the judiciary, the conclusion of studies of various Committees of the Council of Europe is that countries should opt for a 'hierarchical' form of governance involving judges in the relevant decisions. Thus, the Consultative Council of European Judges observed that "over dependence on technology and on those who control it can pose a risk to justice" and that "IT governance should be within the competence of the Council for the judiciary or other equivalent independent body" [16]. Additionally, the European Commission for the Efficiency of Justice considered essential to have a form of centralization, (through a hierarchical model) for successful IT development in the judiciary, though not all member states of the Council of Europe opted for this form of governance [17]. The same advisory body in another report, emphasized the assembly of multidisciplinary teams (technical and legal professionals) "that has real managerial and operational freedom", but also stressed the importance of having a legal professional as a leader who, if necessary, will re-orientate the technical solutions according to the needs of the courts and bearing in mind the legal challenges [18]. Accordingly, the latter report proposed "the adoption of a single, simple, clearly defined system of governance that makes it possible to separate the management of the project from the rest of the administration" and advised the creation of 'temporary' governing bodies with cross-sectoral personnel that operate the court IT system throughout its lifecycle.

The above mentioned works cover either issues of interoperability governance in the private/public sector or the governance structure of the judiciary in the introduction of an ICT project. Our understanding is that the literature is fragmented and is not using a common framework. Usually the authors either introduce a new framework or base their examination in frameworks of other fields. This could lead to inconsistency and is difficult for the reader to thoroughly follow the results of each research. We hold that it is imperative to have a consistent framework to examine interoperability of information systems and we presume that, at least in Europe, EIF 2017 is a good starting point. Regarding the model of governance, there is an agreement to the three basic forms (hierarchy, network and market). In our literature review –that included a sequential investigation of the references of the above mentioned works- we did not identify any case study on the governance structures that the judiciary established in order to promote interoperability, which is the issue we examine in this paper.

3 Methodology

In order to examine the way the competent bodies reached decisions about interoperability issues of IACCMS we used the qualitative technique of case research strategy in studies of information systems [19]. Our aim was both to explore the way the governance structure of IACCMS affected interoperability decisions and validate EIF's 2017 recommendations on this issue.

The unit of analysis is IACCMS; it meets the three criteria for this method to be viable, namely: a) one of the authors, who is an administrative judge in Greece can study IACCMS in its natural setting, b) we can understand the nature and complexity of the processes taking place and c) we examine an area (interoperability in Information Systems of the judiciary) in which few previous studies have been carried out. Moreover, for the chosen unit of analysis the case study research, which aims at the conduct of research, is a more appropriate method than application descriptions, which analyze a researchers' experience in enforcing a particular application, or action research, in which a researcher is both a participant in the actualization of a system and an evaluator of an intervention technique [19].

IACCMS was introduced in Administrative Justice of Greece on 2015. Before that only the Supreme Administrative Court (called Council of State, henceforth, CS) had an integrated case management system. CS, which pursuant to the Greek Constitution has the authority for the management of administrative justice, established an IT Committee consisted of judges and an ICT Division within the registrar of the court consisted of court officers with IT background. The computerization of the rest of administrative courts was fragmented, since each court was perceived (from an IT point of view) as an autonomous entity; that is each court was responsible both for the administration of its data and for the communication with external users (including other administrative courts). Also, there was a lack of IT personnel. The inconsistencies of this fragmentation had as a result the decision to introduce an integrated court case management system for administrative justice.

Therefore, our case study (which is a single-case research) was a unique opportunity to study the governance structure of an IS from planning phase up to the operational phase. It was also a critical case to test EIF 2017 and, essentially, towards building theory in interoperability governance which is still in its developmental stages. IACCMS had a twofold way of dealing with interoperability issues: i) regarding existing IS of administrative courts, an integration of all -formerly isolated- systems into the new one, ii) regarding external IS, the establishment of interoperability. The relevant questions in our case study were: 'what' were the main decisions, 'who' had the mandate to make them and 'how' those decisions were implemented. Those questions also point to the case study as an appropriate research method [19, table 1].

Following the positivism model, our aim was to "generate data which are valid and reliable, independently of the research setting" [20]. We collected data from many sources so as to triangulate the information we derived from them and to support our findings. The data were collected between May 2019 and July 2019 from: a) archival records (in Greek): the public procurement and the contract notice of IACCMS, as well as the contract of 2005 regarding the computerization of eleven administrative courts of first instance (previous IT project in administrative justice), b) documentation (in Greek): the guidelines, via emails, that the Central Organizational Committee (henceforth, COC) issued during the transition and operational phases of IACCMS, the documents (deliverables) that the contractor issued regarding the interoperability of IACCMS and relevant legislation, c) a physical artifact: the Interoperability Quick Assessment Toolkit (IQAT), that was developed from the ISA[2] Program of the European Commission and d) direct observation: due to the fact that one of the authors is an administrative judge in Greece, he was able to observe the day-to-day operation of the system, discussing relevant issues with court officers from the registrar of the court as well as with the president of COC and with a court officer of the ICT Division of the registrar of CS; those discussions were not unstructured (or open-ended) interviews, though the author tried to be 'active listener' and after each discussion he took notes (in Greek) of relevant issues that were clarified; the data from this category represent that author's interpretation of what has been observed.

4 Results

In the following table our findings of the case study are briefly presented. They are thoroughly discussed in the following two subsections, which follow, in a linear way, the phases of the project (Table 1).

Table 1. Matrix of findings

Stakeholders	Decision making process	Legal interoperability	Organizational interoperability
Before initiation of the project			
Political actor	Hierarchy, grant authority, do not interfere	Establish legal framework in which standards are set for all layers/time frame	There is no need for interoperability agreements
Competent centralized authority	Informal collaboration with political actor (goal alignment)		
Planning phase			
Competent centralized authority	Hierarchy, evaluate previous experience and build on existing infrastructure	Use standards set by law	Get users feedback in advance
Piloting phase and operational phase			
Competent centralized authority	Set up new bodies if needed and collaborate. Retain hierarchy in a network structure that facilitates consultation		Goal alignment between organizations and respect independence of organizations

4.1 Before the Initiation of IACCMS (Planning Phase)

The Ministry of Justice, Transparency and Human Rights supervises the administration of justice, dealing with organizational issues, the infrastructure and provides economic (through the budget of the State) and administrative support to the judiciary. It assessed previous ICT projects in administrative justice, consulted with CS and opted for a central governance structure for the planning, procurement, operation and maintenance of IACCMS, without further intervening in the project. It decided that CS would lead the project of introducing a new IS for administrative justice. That political decision had a positive effect in establishing an efficient governance structure for the project and further enabling interoperability. Thus, it is valuable to assess (and learn) from previous ventures before pursuing a new one.

Furthermore, CS had valuable institutional knowledge, since: i) it successfully introduced a case management system for its operations as early as 2006, and ii) it is, pursuant to the Greek Constitution, entitled to oversee the rational operation of administrative justice. Thus, an important lesson is to use an established body with prior experience and the authority (mandate) to lead the project. The knowledge derived from the experience of previous projects –which were introduced, without central coordination and cooperation between courts- was also evident in the decision to build on existing infrastructure, since IACCMS is in essence an evolution of the integrated case management system of CS.

The involved stakeholders (judges and court officers of other administrative courts) generally recognized that a coordinating authority was needed to issue directives and to guide them especially during transition from piloting to operational phase; nearly all stakeholders understood that they would benefit of an integrated public service delivery that IACCMS would provide to administrative justice. However, the 30.03.2015 written communication of the President of CS indicates that not all stakeholders shared the same enthusiasm for IACCMS.

Moreover, an essential lesson is to solve as many issues as possible at the legal level, before implementing a project either for introducing a new IS or further developing an existing one. The Greek Interoperability Framework was introduced with a ministerial decision on 2012. It was compliant with the European Interoperability Framework of 2010. CS has ruled (Opinions 19/2012, 38/2013 and 252/2013 on Presidential Degrees regarding e-justice), that this legal framework does not directly apply to courts, public prosecutors offices and their registrars, though it is useful to be considered on issues of e-justice because it regulates similar issues. Hence, CS decided that IACCMS should be designed in order to be compliant with that particular framework and so there was not a need for drafting interoperability agreements. Thus, there seems to be a correlation between the setting of standards by law and the need for interoperability agreements. It is also useful to enact the relevant legislation that makes an ICT solution mandatory within a specific time frame. Thus, the competent authorities will have a mandate to introduce the new IS within specific boundaries and will also have sufficient time to configure it, test it in a piloting phase, assess the feedback and roll it out. Such an approach will also resolve interoperability problems related to a lack of willingness to collaborate, that some stakeholders may have. Therefore, it is helpful if all users are heard before the relevant legislation is enacted.

4.2 During the Implementation of IACCMS (Piloting and Operational Phases)

Although CS was a key enabler in the new project, it acknowledged, during the piloting phase of the project that it could not sufficiently address all the issues that the other administrative courts had to deal with in order to incorporate IACCMS. There were problems during the transition of existing IS to IACCMS and also during the introduction of IACCMS to courts that did not support an IS.

The General Commission of the State for the Regular Administrative Courts, which is a separate branch of senior administrative judges, monitors the operation of administrative courts and assists them without interfering with their judicial task. It established COC, which was a new informal permanent body that addressed the above described issue. Also, two informal ad hoc Committees, nine informal Committees at the administrative court of appeals and further an informal working group were set up to deal -for a limited period- with specific topics that arose. The lesson is that the governance model should be able to change due to unforeseen issues, that are observed during the piloting phase of an IS or the transition from an older version of an IS to a new one. We therefore understand that 'interoperability governance' is successful when it is 'dynamic' not 'static'. It is a key factor of success to include all stakeholders (in this case through a proxy, COC) in the process of introducing a new IT system, though a leading stakeholder (in this case CS) is needed so as to drive the project forward. In essence, CS provides strategic direction, whereas CS consults COC in issues regarding the other administrative courts so as to coordinate the activities of IACCMS. Our view is that the governance structure of IACCMS is not a duopoly, though it has many aspects of a network, especially when addressing change management and day-to-day management issues; the network aspects of the governance structure were developed because of the issues that had to be addressed during the rolling out of IACCMS. We argue that it is a hybrid structure, since it is flexible enough to establish new temporary or permanent bodies to address issues of greater importance or to realign the management responsibilities between CS and COC. Although the governance structure shifted during the different phases of the project from a decision making perspective it remained a hierarchy. It was the collaboration between COC and CS that established clear and direct communication channels (including regular meetings) during transition from piloting to operational phase of IACCMS. The data we collected point to COC having concurrent competence to take initiatives regarding the implementation of changes to IACCMS at other administrative courts within the goals that CS sets.

Additionally, at the organizational level, interoperability between two IS, is more easily achieved if the incentives of the two organizations are aligned to a mutual goal. In our case study lawyers, judges and court officers were willing to establish a service for the electronic filing of a case. Both IACCMS and the lawyer's portal respected the independence of each other and so the latter portal was built as a single point of access for the lawyers, who upload their files once and the two systems only exchange relevant data. The separate design of the systems renders easier to standardize the relevant processes and also addresses separately maintenance issues. Therefore, tasks are easier attributed when the boundaries of IS are clear. Since parties, after the e-filing of a case, can also submit documents physically to the court, IACCMS provides a multichannel service delivery; it integrates both offline and online channels.

The following figure displays the shifting of the governance structure of IACCMS during the different phases of the project. We assume that in case the IS has to be expanded the same phases will be followed (Fig. 1).

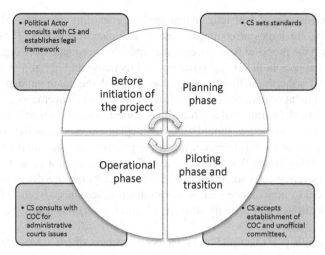

Fig. 1. Governance structure of IACCMS during the phases of the project

5 Discussion

Pertaining to two of our research questions ('who' had the mandate to make the main interoperability decision and 'what' were they), CS is the competent authority to deal with interoperability decisions regarding IACCMS. Judges were members of the IT Committee and the Tender Committee and they made all the relevant decisions, particularly: 1) the decision to centralize and integrate legacy systems in the new IS, 2) the decision to interoperate with external IS by accepting standards regarding technical, semantic and organizational interoperability that had been set via legislation; this finding reveals that there is a trade-off between imposing standards through legislation and drafting interoperability agreements that distribute responsibilities among organizations that want to interoperate and 3) the decision to build on existing infrastructure and expand it; a decision that was consistent with underlying principle 4 of EIF 2017 'reusability'.

Regarding our third research question ('how' the interoperability decisions were implemented), our findings pointed that a strict hierarchy was not able to cope with this issue. During the piloting phase of the project problems –not previously anticipated– revealed themselves and thus the governance structure was altered. There were new informal bodies that were set up and one of them, COC, continued to have a permanent role even after the issues that had to deal with were resolved; regarding interoperability the crucial issue was the introduction of the e-filing of the case from lawyers' portal to IACCMS. Thus, one useful finding is that the way interoperability decisions were introduced (the 'how' question) affected the bodies that were responsible for the decisions (the 'who' question).

We identified as a factor of success of IACCMS, its 'dynamic' governance structure. The governance bodies were not set up at once but they evolved during the life cycle of the project, especially at the time that problems were identified. The introduction of a proxy for all stakeholders (COC) facilitated the rolling out of IACCMS to all administrative courts. However, the governance structure remained a hierarchy since

CS has the final say on all decisions, including those regarding interoperability, though it consults COC for issues affecting the rest of administrative courts. Those findings correspond with the proposal for a governance model to coordinate inter-organizational relationships that uses both vertical governance (hierarchy) and horizontal governance (network) [14]. Furthermore, those findings correlate with the statement that "interoperability in government needs a resilient and flexible model of IT governance, which helps advance the political, institutional and functional opportunities over time" [7]. Still, [15] implies that governance bodies should set up at the planning phase; on the contrary, our findings point to a continuous restructuring of the governance structure in order to deal with interoperability issues that may arise at different phases of a project. Therefore, the model of governance is important and affects interoperability decisions; hence a 'dynamic' model of governance -that is a centralized governance structure (hierarchy) which consults through a proxy with all stakeholders (network)- is better able to address interoperability decisions.

Also our results point that one of the factors of success of IACCMS was the alignment between the aim of the judiciary and a political priority (efficiency of justice) at an early stage. Many stakeholders anticipated an integrated case management system for all administrative courts and the political actor rode the momentum providing the necessary funding. This finding corresponds to EIF's 2017 view [1, Annex 2] that political support is needed for a successful cross-sectoral interoperability project; in our research interoperability between IACCMS and the lawyer's portal for the e-filing of a case. It also corresponds to the first step that [15] proposes. However, we did not identify any recommendations on EIF 2017 regarding the model of governance for interoperability issues, unless one views the term "holistic governance" as encompassing the aforementioned findings. Therefore, our research contributes to building theory and in essence supplementing EIF 2017 on the issue of interoperability governance.

Furthermore, the Ministry of Justice, Transparency and Human Rights enshrined the constitutional guarantee for an independent judiciary and the recommendations from European judiciary organizations that emphasized the importance of having judges actively involved in an ICT project concerning them [16, 17 and 18]. Our findings suggest that the independence of justice is a principle that imposes limitations on the competent authorities (the 'who' question) that make the relevant decisions regarding the interoperability of an IS for the judiciary.

This research could be extended in order to explore governance structures of other IS of the judiciary both inside and outside Greece. Further research could particularly investigate whether apart from a 'dynamic' governance structure, where judges are actively involved, other governance models could successfully be implemented in the introduction of an ICT project in the judiciary, fostering interoperability and without hindering the independence of justice.

6 Conclusions

From the case study we can deductively infer that the 'dynamic' governance structure (agile approach) of IACCMS serves as a strong example for public administrations, especially the judiciary, to model. In this way a centralized authority improves the coordination and efficiency of the network. We conclude that governance, not development, is the most difficult issue to solve. Pursuant to the data we collected our findings suggest it is decisive that the competent authority in the governance structure of an IS has some flexibility in the running of the project, so that, it opts for ad hoc solutions that fulfil the organization's requirements for interoperability. We further affirm the observation of the European Commission for the Efficiency of Justice that: "Changes in the field of cyberjustice should be court-driven, not technology-driven. This implies that organizations must be able to set modernization objectives free from any concerns related to the information technology itself. This is an essential condition for the success of any project, without which there is a risk that it will fail to serve the interests either of those who use the courts or of those who work in them and will, if anything, ultimately undermine confidence in the judiciary as an institution" [18].

References

1. European Commission: Communication from the Commission to the European Parliament, the Council, the European Economic and Social Committee and the Committee of the Regions, European Interoperability Framework – Implementation Strategy, COM(2017) 134 final, Brussels, 23 March 2017
2. Lambropoulou, M., Oikonomou, G.: Theoretical models of public administration and patterns of state reform in Greece. Int. Rev. Adm. Sci. **84**(1), 101–121 (2018). https://doi.org/10.1177/0020852315611219
3. Mongkol, K.: The critical review of new public management model and its criticisms. Res. J. Bus. Manag. **5**(10), 35–43 (2011). https://doi.org/10.3923/rjbm.2011.35.43
4. Leclercq-Vandelannoitte, A., Bertin, E.: From sovereign IT governance to liberal IT governmentality? A Foucauldian analogy. Eur. J. Inf. Syst. **27**(3), 326–346 (2018). https://doi.org/10.1080/0960085X.2018.1473932
5. Weil, P., Ross, J.W.: IT Governance: How Top Performers Manage IT Decision Rights for Superior Results. Harvard Business School Press, Boston (2004)
6. Kooper, M.N., Maes, R., Lindgreen, R.: On the governance of information: introducing a new concept of governance to support the management of information. Int. J. Inf. Manag. **31**(3), 195–200 (2011). https://doi.org/10.1016/j.ijinfomgt.2010.05.009
7. Kubicek, H., Cimander, R., Scholl, H.J.: Organizational Interoperability in E-Government Lessons from 77 European Good-Practice Cases. Springer, Heidelberg (2011). https://doi.org/10.1007/978-3-642-22502-4
8. Estermann, B., Riedl, R., Neuroni A.C.: "Integrated" and "Transcendent" E-government: Keys for Analyzing Organizational Structure and Governance. https://www.researchgate.net/publication/221584693_Integrated_and_transcendent_e-government_keys_for_analyzing_organizational_structure_and_governance. Accessed 02 Sept 2019
9. Provan, K.G., Lemaire, R.H.: Core concepts and key ideas for understanding public sector organizational networks: using research to inform scholarship and practice. Public Adm. Rev. **72**(5), 638–648 (2012). http://doi.org/10.111/j.1540-6210.2012.02595.x
10. Wimmer, M.A., Boneva, R., di Giacomo, D.: Interoperability governance: a definition and insights from case studies in Europe. In: DG.O 2018: Proceedings of the 19th Annual International Conference on Digital Government Research, 30 May–1 June 2018. Delft University of Technology, Delft (2018). https://doi.org/10.1145/3209281.3209306
11. Sundberg, L.: Enablers for interoperability in decentralized e-government settings. In: DG.O 2018: Proceedings of the 19th Annual International Conference on Digital Government Research, 30 May–1 June 2018. Delft University of Technology, Delft (2018). https://doi.org/10.1145/3209281.3209303

12. Scholl, H.J., Alawadhi, S.: Creating smart governance: the key to radical ICT overhaul at the City of Munich. Inf. Polity **21**(1), 21–42 (2016). https://doi.org/10.3233/IP-150369

13. Nielsen, M.M.: Governance lessons from Denmark's digital transformation. In: DG.O 2019: Proceedings of the 20th Annual International Conference on Digital Government Research, 18 June–20 June 2019, pp. 456–461. Mohammed Bin Rashid School of Government Dubai, United Arab Emirates (2019). https://doi.org/10.1145/3325112.3329881

14. Boudreau, C., Bernier, L.: The implementation of integrated electronic service delivery in Quebec: the conditions of collaboration and lessons. Int. Rev. Adm. Sci. **83**(3), 602–620 (2017). https://doi.org/10.1177/0020852315598215

15. European Commission: EIF Roadmap. How to deliver a new integrated public service. https://joinup.ec.europa.eu/collection/nifo-national-interoperability-framework-observatory/document/eif-infographic-roadmap-developing-new-integrated-public-service. Accessed 10 Mar 2020

16. Council of Europe, Consultative Council of European Judges: Opinion No.(2011)14 of the CCJE "Justice and information technologies (IT)", Adopted by the CCJE at its 12th plenary meeting (Strasbourg, 7–9 November 2011), CCJE(2011)2 Final

17. Council of Europe, European Commission for the Efficiency of Justice: The use of the information technologies in European courts - CEPEJ Studies No. 24, adopted by the CEPEJ at its 27th plenary meeting (Strasbourg, 30 June–1 July 2016). https://rm.coe.int/european-judicial-systems-efficiency-and-quality-of-justice-cepej-stud/1680788229. Accessed 02 Sept 2019

18. Council of Europe, European Commission for the Efficiency of Justice: Guidelines on how to drive change towards Cyberjustice. Stock-taking of tools deployed and summary of good practices, as adopted at the 28th meeting of the CEPEJ on 7 December 2016. https://edoc.coe.int/en/efficiency-of-justice/7501-guidelines-on-how-to-drive-change-towards-cyberjustice-stock-taking-of-tools-deployed-and-summary-of-good-practices.html. Accessed 02 Sept 2019

19. Benbasat, I., Goldstein, D.K., Mead, M.: The case research strategy in studies of information systems. MIS Q. **11**(3), 369–386 (1987)

20. Silverman, D.: Interpreting Qualitative Data, 5th edn. Sage, Los Angeles, London, New Delhi, Singapore, Washington DC (2014)

Making e-Government Work: Learning from the Netherlands and Estonia

Nitesh Bharosa[1]([⊠])[iD], Silvia Lips[2][iD], and Dirk Draheim[2][iD]

[1] Digicampus, Delft University of Technology, Delft, The Netherlands
n.bharosa@tudelft.nl
[2] Information Systems Group, Tallinn University of Technology, Tallinn, Estonia
{silvia.lips,dirk.draheim}@taltech.ee

Abstract. Countries are struggling to develop data exchange infrastructures needed to reap the benefits of e-government. Understanding the development of infrastructures can only be achieved by combining insights from institutional, technical and process perspectives. This paper contributes by analysing data exchange infrastructures in the Netherlands and Estonia from an integral perspective. The institutional design framework of Koppenjan and Groenewegen is used to analyse the developments in both countries. The analysis shows that the starting points, cultures, path dependencies and institutional structure result in different governance models for data exchange infrastructures. Estonia has a single – centrally governed – data-exchange infrastructure that is used by public and private parties for all kinds of data exchanges (including citizen-to-business and business-to-business). In contrast, the institutional structure in the Netherlands demands a strict demarcation between public and private infrastructures, resulting in several data exchange infrastructures. While there are examples of sharing infrastructure components across various levels of the Dutch government, public infrastructures cannot be used for business-to-business or citizen-to-business data exchange due to the potential for market distortion by government. Both the centrally governed Estonian model and the decentrally governed Dutch model have pros and cons on multiple levels.

Keywords: E-government · Data-exchange infrastructures ·
Institutional design

1 Introduction

Across the globe, demands on public services are increasing at a fast pace, partly due to the widespread availability of new technologies and higher expectations from digitally-savvy citizens. Citizens expect personalized customer journeys at all levels of government, as they have become accustomed to smartphone-empowered lives [1]. New digital data exchange infrastructure are essential for broader service access as well as the provision of significant benefits to service

S. Hofmann et al. (Eds.): ePart 2020, LNCS 12220, pp. 41–53, 2020.
https://doi.org/10.1007/978-3-030-58141-1_4

users at a reduced cost. However, even large budgets are no guarantee for successful digital government transformations [2,3]. From a purely technological perspective, all of this is hard to explain.

This paper argues that, in order to understand what contributes to the success of e-government, we also need to consider the institutional design as well as the design process of developing data-exchange infrastructure. Aiming to learn from successful examples, this paper conducts a comparative case study on two leading countries in e-government: the Netherlands and Estonia. Both the Netherlands and Estonia are in the group of high performers in the e-Government Development Index [4], and both countries have widely adopted data exchange infrastructures [5,6], enabling for instance a pre-filled tax return form that takes minutes to electronically check and submit. For the sake of this paper, a data exchange infrastructure is defined as *the whole of standards, technical components, services and governance framework in place for data exchange*. These are by nature socio-technical constructs [7,8], which makes them hard to understand from a single point of view. Data exchange infrastructures are essential when it comes to the successful delivery of e-government services, since they facilitate process, application and data integration across the various government silos. Therefore, the maturity of data exchange infrastructure can be used as a proxy for e-government maturity.

While there is a growing body of knowledge on the technical design and the governance of data exchange infrastructures, we lack insights from a combined institutional, technical and process perspective. The goal of this paper is to analyse the development of data exchange infrastructures from such a combined design perspective. We conduct the comparative case study by adopting the theoretical framework for multi-facet design of socio-technical systems by Koppenjan and Groenewegen [9]. Koppenjan and Groenwegen state: "Institutions concern different levels of analysis like laws and regulations as well as contracts and organisations which regulate and coordinate the behaviour of actors in complex networks" [9]. Therefore, the framework is suitable for analysing complex socio-technical situations for policy making.

This paper proceeds as follows. Section 2 describes the research approach, which centres around a four day workshop in Estonia. Section 3 discusses the theoretical analysis framework of Koppenjan and Groenewegen that we use to compare data exchange infrastructure policies in the Netherlands and Estonia. Section 4 provides a high-level description of the selected cases the Netherlands and Estonia with respect to their e-government background. The findings of this paper are discussed in Sect. 5. Section 6 concludes the paper and provides recommendations for policy makers.

2   Research Approach

To analyse the development of data exchange infrastructures, we conduct a comparative case-study on the design of the data exchange infrastructures in the Netherlands and Estonia. The research draws on an international collaboration

Table 1. Overview of the workshop in Tallinn, Estonia.

Aspect	Details
Date	18-21 November 2019
Location	Tallinn University of Technology
Participants	The Netherlands: 14 participants (8 policy makers, 3 researchers, 3 software providers) Estonia: 11 participants (4 policy makers, 5 researchers, 2 software providers)
Agenda (high level)	Day 1: Presentations on the current e-government designs and future challenges in both countries Day 2: Working sessions on the challenges surrounding digital identities and e-government Day 3: Working sessions on the countries' data exchange infrastructures. Role playing game on self-sovereign identities in the future Day 4: Reflection, updating the common collaboration agenda, prioritizing collaborative research questions
Data collection methods	Workshop notes, role playing game, Mentimeter, collective agenda writing

facilitated by Digicampus[1], a quadruple-helix-based innovation partnership for public service innovation in the Netherlands. One of the missions of Digicampus is to facilitate international collaboration on designing the next generation of public services. One of the vehicles for realizing this is an international collaboration agenda, focusing on current issues in e-government, learning from each other's e-government agendas and pinpointing topics that are suited for collaborative research and prototyping. The first concrete research activity as part of this agenda was a four-day workshop in Tallinn from November 18 to 21, 2019. Table 1 provides an overview of this workshop.

3   The Theoretical Analysis Framework

Koppenjan and Groenwegen [9] introduce an analysis framework for a certain class of large-scale technological systems that do not consist merely out of technological assets, but involve institutions as part of their solutions. Institutions regulate behaviour and are essential components of socio-technical systems. Socio-technical systems are characterized by their complexity due to the many dependencies between the institutional and technology parts shaped by change processes. Koppenjan and Groenwegen suggested to analyze such system as a technological design that is teamed together with an institutional design [10],

---

[1] www.digicampus.tech.

see Fig. 1 ("co-design perspective"). Moreover, they suggest to make the design
of the design process (*process design*) explicit in the analysis of such system (the
design process in Fig. 1 is simply the process that yields the technological design
and the institutional design, the *process design* is actually a '*design process*'
design). For our purposes, it is important to understand all designs (technological design, institutional design and process design) as continuously recurring
endeavours that evolve and improve over time. Now, technological design is about
"demarcation, components, relations, processes" [9] of/in the technological system; institutional design is about "arrangements between actors that regulate
their relations: tasks, responsibilities, allocation of costs, benefits and risks" [9];
process design is about "who participates in the design process; what are the
conditions, rules, roles, items, steps, etc." [9].

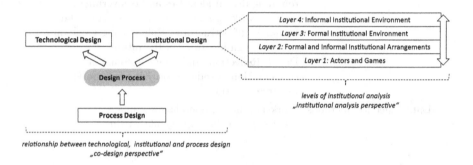

Fig. 1. A institutional design model by Koppenjan and Groenewegen [9].

In order to adequately grasp institutional design, Koppenjan and Groenewegen introduce a second perspective that adapts Williamson's four-layer model of
economics of institutions [11], see again Fig. 1 ("institutional analysis perspective"). Layer 4 is the layer of the "*informal* institutional environment of socio-
technical systems", which is about "norms, values, orientation, codes (informal institutions, culture)" [9], see also [12], compare with [13]. Layer 3 is the
layer of the "*formal* institutional environment" [9], which is about "formal rules,
laws and regulations, constitutions (formal institutions)" [9], see also [14], compare with [15]. Layer 2 is the layer of the "*formal and informal* institutional
arrangements" [9], which is about "gentleman agreements, covenants, contracts,
alliances, joint-ventures, merges, etc." [9] and informal "rules, codes, norms, orientation, relations" [9], see also [16], compare with [17]. Layer 1 is the layer
of the "actors and games" [9], which is about "actors/agents and their interactions aimed at creating and influencing (infrastructural) provisions, services,
outcomes" [9], compare with [18]. The systems that Koppenjan and Groenewegen address are large-scale systems: "energy networks, water management services [...], waste treatment, transport systems (rail, road, water, tube), industrial networks, information systems and telecommunication networks, city service" [9]. Information systems are among those systems, however, the model

becomes actually relevant only if an information system is beyond the scope of usual enterprise architecture [19], i.e., involves an ultra-large-scale software system [20]. Therefore, e-government systems are typical instances of the system class characterized by the model of Koppenjan and Groenewegen [9], the model is a suitable candidate as an analysis framework for e-government systems, e-government ecosystems and interoperability solutions alike. This is why we have chosen the model as the theoretical basis of our comparative case study. In our analysis, we exploit both the perspective of relationships between technological/institutional/process design (that we call "co-design perspective" for short) and the four-layered model of institutional design (that we call "institutional analysis perspective" for short).

4   Background in the Netherlands and Estonia

4.1   The Netherlands

The Netherlands consistently performs well in e-government rankings [4]. The country has a high level of decentralized governance and public private collaboration in public service delivery. This decentralization results into various government agencies that use different infrastructures. For instance, the Tax administration uses a different data exchange infrastructure with the private sector and other government agencies (called Digipoort) [21] than the customs authority (called Single Window for Maritime and Aviation) [22]. Across different sectors such as health, energy and education, different data exchange infrastructures are used. Table 2 provides an (incomplete) overview of the main data exchange infrastructures in the Netherlands.

Table 2 is by no means exhaustive, but does highlight the variety in data exchange infrastructures. While some are only web-portal based, most infrastructures support application-to-application data exchange. Municipalities also have different infrastructures, which provides autonomy, but is not cheap to operate and maintain. On a municipal level, there is a growing tendency to combine forces and to develop and use a shared infrastructure. Inspired by the X-Road approach in Estonia, municipalities are currently piloting with the "common ground".

4.2   Estonia

Estonia is signee of the D9 (Digital Nine) charter, i.e., a member of the "Digital Nations" network, also known as D9 or "Leading Digital Governments". In media, on international conventions on digital transformation as well as in policy maker circles it is often perceived or presents itself as leader when it comes to e-government; actually, stakeholder from many countries, as from the Netherlands, have visited Estonia with the aim to learn from their success. The perception of Estonia as a digital leader might be, in large parts, due to communication strategy [23] and nation branding [24]; still: the technological, legal and

Table 2. Overview of various data exchange infrastructures in the Netherlands.

Sector	Data exchange infrastructure
Citizen-to-government interaction	MijnOverheid (mijn.overheid.nl, also available as an app) is the national citizen portal with access to the online citizen message box + rerouting to multiple agency specific portals (e.g. social services, unemployment services, tax, municipal portal). With the exception of pension funds, businesses cannot use this portal (or the app) for data exchange with citizens
Government to government data exchange (G2G)	Diginetwerk (logius.nl/diensten/diginetwerk) includes multiple networks, including municipal data exchange, base registers access and social services
Financial reporting: B2G (business-to-government) and G2G	Digipoort (logius.nl/diensten/digipoort) is the government data exchange gateway including multiple services (i.e. authentication, authorisation, validation and archiving). Since Digipoort may not be used for B2B data exchange, there is private sector counterpart (Bancaire Infrastructurele Voorziening) with similar functionalities
Trade & transport	Single Window for Maritime and Aviation (kvnr.nl/en/msw) for all communications intended for Customs and the Royal Netherlands Marechaussee / Seaport Police can be communicated electronically
Public health services	Landelijk Schakelpunt (vzvz.nl/over-het-lsp) for data exchange in the medical domain
Mortgages	Mortgages Data Network (HDN.nl) for data exchange in the mortgages domain

organizational assets in Estonia have been designed with and for each other and evolved over time into a particularly stable e-government ecosystem. At the centre of the Estonian e-government ecosystem lies the interoperability framework X-Road [5, 25]. Estonia created X-Road – an application network for exchanging data among agency systems so that all government services are effectively available in one spot. In addition to offering querying mechanisms across multiple databases and supporting the secure exchange of documents [26], X-Road seamlessly integrates different government portals and applications. Also the private sector can also connect with X-Road to make queries and benefit from access to a secure data exchange layer [27].

5 Findings

The main objective of the workshop in Estonia was to learn from each other's approaches to e-government design and look ahead which challenges could be dealt with in a collaborative manner. Table 3 outlines the comparison based on the layered institutional analysis of the institutional design model of Koppenjan and Groenewegen [9].

Table 3. Institutional analysis based on the Koppenjan and Groenewegen model [9].

Layer	The Netherlands	Estonia
Layer 4: Informal institutional environment	Government is trusted and consist of reliable institutions to meet performance expectations. Strong boundaries between public agencies and the private sector, yet long tradition in public-private collaboration	Government is trusted [28,29] and consist of reliable institutions to meet performance expectations. Open interaction between public agencies and the private sector
Layer 3: Formal institutional environment	Legislation focused on public agency tasks (e.g. tax and customs laws) as well as laws on interactions with public agencies. No law on e-government in place yet (although a draft)	Exhaustive set of stable legal assets that are designed with respect to (resp. co-designed with) the technological assets of the e-government ecosystem
Layer 2: Formal and informal institutional agreements	Decentralized steering of e-government. High level of autonomy across various levels of government. Moderate focus on economies of scale (e.g., the use of Digipoort by four government agencies, but not by banks for business-to-business data exchange), focus on administrative reduction by citizens and the public	Centralized steering of e-government. Whole-of-government approach to modernize service delivery in a joined-up manner. Strong focus on economies of scale: the use of state eID, national registries and X-Road for both public and private services. Focus on creating transparency by showing all transactions
Layer 1: Actors and games	Innovation is largely left to the market, strong emphasis on innovation by the private sector through outsourcing and grants (e.g., startups). Large enterprises are incentivized by the business potential when winning a multi-year service delivery tender. Innovation in the private sector is stimulated, but government is risk-averse and no knowledge and capacity building at the government	Innovation by government for the entire society. Central government carries risks of innovation, strong emphasis on innovation and service delivery by government agencies. Experimentation by the government is stimulated and in this way knowledge and understanding of the public and technology is created

Table 4. Institutional comparison from the co-design perspective (Koppenjan and Groenewegen [9]).

	The Netherlands	Estonia
Technological design	Multiple digital infrastructures (mix of state-owned and -sourced as a service from the market). State-owned or -sourced infrastructures cannot be used for citizen-to-business or business-to-business data exchange	Single, state-owned and -operated digital infrastructure (X-Road), which can be used for all kinds of e-services, including citizen-to-business and business-to-business data exchange. Strong focus on economies of scale: the use of state eID, national registries and X-Road for both public and private services
Process design	Fragmented and loosely coordinated agency and sector-specific resource allocation and decision-making. Various national and local e-government and digital innovation agendas. Strong emphasis on the consultation of the private sector (i.e., software vendors) in the design and pre-procurement process. Coordination by having a standardization list and government architecture	Tightly coordinated decision-making and resource allocation for e-government (CIO office) based on a whole-of-government approach for achieving synergies. Focus on implementing shared design principles, including once-only and full transparency in data usage
Institutional design	Highly autonomous government institutions. Separation of government agencies that create policy, deliver services and supervision agencies. Government agencies cannot compete with private enterprises in service delivery. There is a law that prohibits government agencies from developing digital technologies or services that are already available in the market	Well-orchestrated government institutions. Regulated interplay of government agencies that create policy, deliver services and supervision agencies. Service provisioning is streamlined by a central authority. Government prototypes architectures for emerging challenges itself

During the workshops, multiple user/citizen oriented contexts were used to compare the e-governments in Estonia and the Netherlands: using the life event approach [30], user-centred scenarios were discussed in depth, specifically comparing the steps users need to take in order to achieve their goals. This provided rich case descriptions as substance for the institutional analysis

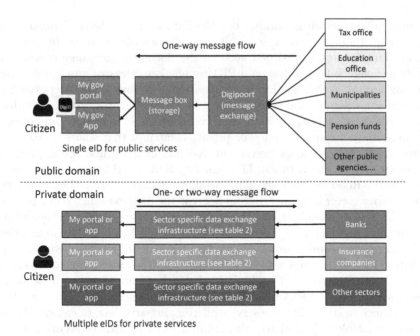

Fig. 2. High-level technical design of the Dutch data exchange infrastructures (please note that not all the different infrastructures outlined in Table 2 are displayed).

frameworks. Next, Table 4 outlines the comparison based on the technological/institutional/process co-design perspective of the institutional design model of Koppenjan and Groenewegen [9].

The high-level technical design of the Dutch data exchange infrastructures is sketched in Fig. 2.

In accordance with Table 2, citizens work with multiple data exchange infrastructures in the Netherlands. The demarcation is clear for public services and private services. When consuming public services, citizens can use the state-issued eID called DigID (digid.nl/en). The 'MijnOverheid' portal and app provides data access to public agency messages (pdf files). This is a one-way data flow; for service consumption or data entry users need to go to the website/portal of the respective public agency. Here, they can use DigID. Since law dictates that DigID (as well as other public sector data exchange infrastructure components such as the 'MijnOverheid' portal and app, the citizen message box and the Digipoort) can only be used by public organizations, private organizations have to use their own infrastructure or use sector-specific infrastructures (see Table 2 for an overview).

The high-level technical design of the Estonian data exchange infrastructure is sketched in Fig. 3. Estonia embraces an integrated design, which extends the technology. X-Road consists of technical, legal and organizational assets that are teamed together as described in the sequel. In a narrow sense, the data exchange infrastructure is nothing but the data exchange layer X-Road (dark grey in Fig. 2); in a broader sense, it encompasses also crosscutting services that are built on top of X-Road such as the document exchange center [26]. The data exchange layer relies on a PKI (public key infrastructure) and a time stamping service. A PKI is itself a combination of technological assets (such as the certification server) and an institution, i.e., the CA (certification authority). Next, the X-Road consists of security servers, which are software components. Each organization (public agency or private company) that wants to exchange messages over X-Road must become an X-Road member first, by application and registration at the Estonian IT Authority RIA (Riigi Infosüsteemi Amet). Then, each X-Road member needs to install the security server. The basic task of the security server is to encrypt and decrypt the data exchange messages sent among the X-Road members. For this, the security server teams together with a signature device, which must be obtained from the CA by each X-Road member. Furthermore, the security server allows for access rights management: each X-Road member can determine itself, which other X-Road members can access its services. It is regulated that each X-Road member announces its information systems and services to RIA before it is allowed to launch them. This way, RIA has the chance to streamline the service offering, in particular, to enforce the the once-only principle [31]. Similarly, timestamping by the installed security servers as well as timestamping service provision are subject to regulations. All citizens can see all communications about them. This creates transparency and ensures that mistakes or fraud can be detected immediately.

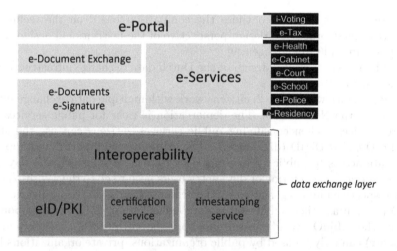

Fig. 3. High level, integrated technical design of the Estonian data exchange infrastructure.

The Estonian e-government ecosystem is a network consisting of different players with well-defined roles. As a fundamental task, the e-government ecosystem implements the Estonian eID [28,32], which provides also the basis for any system interoperability, compare again with Fig. 2. The Information System Authority (RIA) and the Estonian Police and Border Guard Board (PBGB) are the main authorities in the e-government ecosystem. RIA[2] operates on behalf of the Ministry of Economic Affairs and Communications[3]. RIA coordinates the development and administration of the state's information system. It oversees the functioning of the Estonian PKI, organizes activities related to information security, handles security incidents that occur in Estonian computer networks, and serves as the technical eID competence centre.

6   Conclusions and Policy Recommendations

Estonia and the Netherlands had different starting points and used different paths in developing their e-government. The main differences in approaching e-government boil down in the following categories:

- Strong centralized government institutions in Estonia versus decentralized and market-oriented institutions in the Netherlands.
- Institutional boundaries in the Netherlands between the use of state-owned digital infrastructures (or components) for public services (only allowed for citizen-to-government interactions) and semi/non-public services (not allowed for citizen-to-business and business-to-business interactions) versus no boundary in Estonia (single infrastructure, seamless use across public and private services).
- Focus on experimenting and learning by doing in Estonia, whereas the Netherlands is risk-averse and leaves innovation to the market.

These differences make it difficult to copy each other best practices as the institutional settings are different, and due to the different data exchange infrastructures that are currently in place. Nevertheless, both countries can learn from each other's approaches. The capacity of reliable institutions to meet performance expectations, perceptions of competence and effective public service delivery for all, along with public accountability, should be among the leading concerns in developing e-government further. It is recommended that governments exploit the potential of digital technologies through coherent national policies that are closely aligned with the knowledge of user needs that is available at the respective public agencies. Being successful requires a whole-of-government approach across ministries and agencies and between levels, as well as partnerships with non-government actors. Such an approach needs to be supported by a high-level political will, an example of which is an effective cross-government institution with clearly earmarked financial resources and decision-making powers. This demands a shift from inward, disjointed and process-oriented organizational structures to highly collaborative frameworks for seamless delivery of services towards citizens and entrepreneurs. Maximizing the potential of digital

---

[2] https://www.ria.ee/en/.
[3] https://www.mkm.ee/en.

technologies also demands appropriate data exchange infrastructures for interoperability and digital transactions across the public sector, dependent on common standards, data sharing, highly skilled staff, as well as knowledgeable organizational capacity.

References

1. Lemke, F., Taveter, K., Erlenheim, R., Pappel, I., Draheim, D., Janssen, M.: Stage models for moving from e-government to smart government. In: Chugunov, A., Khodachek, I., Misnikov, Y., Trutnev, D. (eds.) EGOSE 2019. CCIS, vol. 1135, pp. 152–164. Springer, Cham (2020). https://doi.org/10.1007/978-3-030-39296-3_12
2. Wonglimpiyarat, J.: Innovative policies to support technology and ICT development. Gov. Inf. Q. **31**(3), 466–475 (2014)
3. OECD: Building organisational capacity for public sector innovation - background paper. In: Proceedings of the OECD Conference "Innovating the Public Sector: From Ideas to Impact" (2014)
4. European Commission: Digital Economy and Society Index (DESI) Report on Digital Public Services 2019 (2019)
5. Kalja, A.: The first ten years of X-Road. In: Kastehein, K., (ed.) Estonian Information Society Yearbook 2011/2012. Ministry of Economic Affairs and Communications of Estonia, pp. 78–80 (2012)
6. Robles, G., Gamalielsson, J., Lundell, B.: Setting up Government 3.0 solutions based on open source software: the case of X-Road. In: Lindgren, I., Janssen, M., Lee, H., Polini, A., Rodríguez Bolívar, M.P., Scholl, H.J., Tambouris, E. (eds.) EGOV 2019. LNCS, vol. 11685, pp. 69–81. Springer, Cham (2019). https://doi.org/10.1007/978-3-030-27325-5_6
7. Tilson, D., Lyytinen, K., Sørensen, C.: Digital infrastructures: the missing IS research agenda. Inf. Syst. Res. **21**(4), 748–759 (2010)
8. Thurnay, L., Klasche, B., Nyman-Metcalf, K., Pappel, I., Draheim, D.: The potential of the Estonian e-governance infrastructure in supporting displaced Estonian residents. In: Kő, A., Francesconi, E. (eds.) EGOVIS 2017. LNCS, vol. 10441, pp. 236–250. Springer, Cham (2017). https://doi.org/10.1007/978-3-319-64248-2_17
9. Koppenjan, J., Groenewegen, J.: Institutional design for complex technological systems. Int. J. Technol. Policy Manage. **5**(3), 240–257 (2005)
10. Goodin, R.: The Theory of Institutional Design. Cambridge University Press, Cambridge (1996)
11. Williamson, O.: Transaction cost economics: how it works; where it is headed. De Economist **146**, 23–58 (1998)
12. Groenewegen, J.: Who should control the firm? Insights from new and original institutional economics. J. Econ. Issues **38**(2), 353–361 (2004)
13. Denzau, A., North, D.: Shared mental models: ideologies and institutions. Kyklos Int. Rev. Soc. Sci. **47**(1), 3–31 (1994)
14. Groenewegen, J.: Transaction Cost Economics and Beyond. Kluwer Academic Publishers, Dordrecht (1996)
15. Olson, M.: The Logic of Collective Action. Public Goods and the Theory of Groups. Harvard University Press, Cambridge (1965)
16. Kickert, W., Klijn, E., Koppenjan, J.: Managing Complex Networks: Strategies for the Public Sector. Sage, Thousand Oaks (1997)

17. Williamson, O.E.: Transaction cost economics: the governance of contractual relations. J. Law Econ. **22**(2), 233–261 (1979)
18. Coase, R.H.: The nature of the firm. Economica **4**(16), 86–405 (1937)
19. Zachman, J.: A framework for information systems architecture. IBM Syst. J. **26**(3), 276–292 (1987)
20. Northrop, L., et al.: Ultra-Large-Scale Systems: The Software Challenge of the Future. Carnegie Mellon University, Software Engineering Institute (2006)
21. Bharosa, N., Wijk, R.V., Winne, N.D., Janssen, M.: Challenging the Chain - Governing the Automated Exchange and Processing of Business Information. IOS Press, Amsterdam (2015)
22. Klievink, B., Bharosa, N., Tan, Y.: The collaborative realization of public values and business goals: governance and infrastructure of public-private information platforms. Gov. Inf. Q. **33**(1), 67–79 (2016)
23. Drechsler, W.: Pathfinder: e-Estonia as the β-version. JeDEM eJournal eDemocracy Open Gov. **10**(2), 1–22 (2018)
24. Kimmo, M., Pappel, I., Draheim, D.: E-residency as a nation branding case. In: Proceedings of ICEGOV 2018: The 11th International Conference on Theory and Practice of Electronic Governance, pp. 419–428. ACM (2018)
25. Mcbride, K., Kütt, A., Yahia, S.B., Draheim, D.: On positive feedback loops in digital government architecture. In: Proceedings of MEDES'2019 - the 11th International Conference on Management of Digital EcoSystems. ACM (2019)
26. Draheim, D., Koosapoeg, K., Lauk, M., Pappel, I., Pappel, I., Tepandi, J.: The design of the Estonian governmental document exchange classification framework. In: Kő, A., Francesconi, E. (eds.) EGOVIS 2016. LNCS, vol. 9831, pp. 33–47. Springer, Cham (2016). https://doi.org/10.1007/978-3-319-44159-7_3
27. Paide, K., Pappel, I., Vainsalu, H., Draheim, D.: On the systematic exploitation of the Estonian data exchange layer X-Road for strengthening public private partnerships. In: Proceedings of ICEGOV 2018 - The 11th International Conference on Theory and Practice of Electronic Governance, pp. 34–41. ACM (2018)
28. Muldme, A., Pappel, I., Lauk, M., Draheim, D.: A survey on customer satisfaction in national Electronic ID user support. In: Proceedings of ICEDEG 2018 - The 5th International Conference on eDemocracy & eGovernment, pp. 31–37. IEEE (2018)
29. Lips, S., Pappel, I., Tsap, V., Draheim, D.: Key factors in coping with large-scale security vulnerabilities in the eID field. In: Kő, A., Francesconi, E. (eds.) EGOVIS 2018. LNCS, vol. 11032, pp. 60–70. Springer, Cham (2018). https://doi.org/10.1007/978-3-319-98349-3_5
30. Wimmer, M.: A European perspective towards online one-stop government: the eGOV project. Electron. Commer. Res. Appl. **1**(1), 92–103 (2002)
31. Wimmer, M., Tambouris, E., Krimmer, R., Gil-Garcia, J., Chatfield, A.T.: Once only principle: benefits, barriers & next steps. In: Proceedings of dg.o 2017 - The 18th Annual International Conference on Digital Government, pp. 602–603. ACM (2017)
32. Tsap, V., Pappel, I., Draheim, D.: Key success factors in introducing national e-identification systems. In: Dang, T.K., Wagner, R., Küng, J., Thoai, N., Takizawa, M., Neuhold, E.J. (eds.) FDSE 2017. LNCS, vol. 10646, pp. 455–471. Springer, Cham (2017). https://doi.org/10.1007/978-3-319-70004-5_33

Theoretical Foundations for the Study of Social Innovation in the Public Sector

Thomas M. Vogl$^{(\boxtimes)}$ (iD)

University of Oxford, Oxford OX1 3JS, UK
thomas.vogl@oii.ox.ac.uk

Abstract. Over the past two decades, there have been significant debates around the theoretical foundations for the study of social and material implications of technological change in organizational settings. Various scholars have looked at these foundations with a focus on either the social and the material as discrete entities, the social and the material as interactive, the sociomaterial as a concept representing the constitutive entanglement of the two, or the sociomaterial as imbricated but analytically distinct. These debates sometimes lead to statements about which foundations are the most appropriate upon which to build studies; however, it may be more productive to delineate what each theoretical foundation affords for the study of social innovation. This paper sets out the affordances of each perspective for the design and execution of research into technologically supported social innovation in the public sector. It provides relevant examples from child protection services to illustrate where and how these different theoretical foundations help researchers to understand phenomena associated with social innovation. In so doing, this paper seeks to clarify the diverse approaches to the study of technologically supported social innovation, their assumptions, and where they may be adopted most effectively.

Keywords: Technological change · Public administration · Social innovation · Social and material · Theoretical foundations

1 Introduction

This paper aims to help moderate the sometimes heated debates around the theoretical foundations for research on the impact of technological change in organizations. Its objective is to set out a framework within which to better understand where different theoretical foundations are more or less useful for particular questions about social innovation in the context of public administration technological change. This paper will also provide examples to illustrate how these theoretical foundations can be applicable to the study of public sector organizational settings.

The hope is that this work will also allow for better scrutiny of when something is a true social innovation, when there is a failure of social innovation, and when something is simply the '#innobasics', or something that government talks about as innovation,

© IFIP International Federation for Information Processing 2020
Published by Springer Nature Switzerland AG 2020
S. Hofmann et al. (Eds.): ePart 2020, LNCS 12220, pp. 54–65, 2020.
https://doi.org/10.1007/978-3-030-58141-1_5

when it is actually something that people just come to expect as the most fundamental components of a technological change [16]. For example: "Making a website that works well for its users at a reasonable cost in a reasonable timeframe. ... That's not innovation. That's just how tech works today. ... Of course, what is innovative today becomes tomorrow's basics." [16]. Ideally, we would like to analytically distinguish when basic technological expectations masquerade as innovation and when things that are considered basic in the private sector are innovatively deployed in the public sector.

This paper is structured as follows: Sect. 2 sets out five predominant theoretical foundations from the literature, including techno-centric, human-centred, social and material interaction, sociomaterial assemblages, and sociomaterial imbrication. Section 2 concludes with a summary of the characteristics of these foundational theoretical perspectives. Section 3 provides some illustrative examples of how these five theoretical foundations can be productively used to answer important questions, while also setting out their limitations. It will then summarize where and when these theoretical foundations are most effective, as well as what assumptions need to be recognized. Section 4 discusses how these perspectives help illuminate different elements of social innovation in different use cases and what this means for the study of technological change and social innovation overall. Section 5 concludes with some thoughts about the applicability of these perspectives to social innovation in the context of public sector technological change and the opportunities they present for the design of future research.

2 Foundational Theoretical Perspectives

There are five predominant foundational theoretical perspectives for the study of information technology in organizations and society, each has its own unique characteristics that distinguish it from the others, but each has a focus on either the material, social, or some combination of both. Prior debates about these perspectives often pitted them against each other in an effort to identify a dominant foundation. But it is possible to take a slightly different approach, focusing on the strength of a given perspective for the study of particular aspects of technological change in organizations, while illustrating how competing perspectives are not wrong, but useful in addressing different types of questions [8]. This approach will be applied here to the five theoretical perspectives, in order to illustrate where these perspectives could be most effectively adopted.

The first three perspectives are theoretical foundations which focus either primarily on the material or the social or the interaction between the two separate constructs [15]. The fourth is a sociomaterial perspective grounded in agential realism, which posits that the material and the social cannot be seen as separate, but only as an assemblage that is revealed through the performativity of practice [13, 14]. The fifth is a sociomaterial perspective grounded in critical realism that permits an analytical dualism between the material and the social, while nevertheless recognizing their imbrication [8].

2.1 Techno-Centric Perspective

The first perspective is from an empirical realist position that looks at the discrete material impact of information technology on organizational factors. This perspective has discrete entities as its ontological priority [15]. Under this perspective, technology is seen as either an independent variable impacting directly on organizational characteristics [15], or as a variable that moderates the relationship between organizational elements and more strategic organizational characteristics [15].

The main criticisms of this perspective are that the empirical results are mixed and that this may be the result of inadequate theoretical foundations [15]. In addition, perspectives like this "entail conceptual commitments that generate some distinctive blindspots in dealing with technology in organizational life" [15]. In particular, an approach that looks at the discrete material impact of information technology on organizational characteristics "suggests that technology is relevant to organizational theorizing only as specific technological events or processes occur" [15]. Further, this techno-centric perspective "reifies technology, ignores how technology is bound up with historical and cultural influences, and thus produces technologically deterministic claims about the relationship of technology with organizations" [14].

2.2 Human-Centred Perspective

The second perspective is from an empirical relativist position that looks at how discrete social factors shape technology. This approach has an ontological commitment to social phenomena and tends to prioritize epistemology and how social phenomena shape what we know about, and how we understand, technology [10, 12]. Under this perspective, interpretivism is adopted to better understand how social factors shape technologies in particular circumstances, as well as how they inform a multidirectional model of technological development [10]. Social shaping recognizes the social impact on technology as well as the mutually constituting relationship that exists, where technology does impose some influence on the social through its materiality [12].

The main criticisms of this perspective are that social factors are assumed to be discrete independent entities with inherent characteristics [15]. Further, social constructivism and social shaping are seen to ignore the consequences of technological choices, focus on 'relevant' social groups to the exclusion of other groups that are impacted by technological choices, and neglect the structural elements of the technologies that are so shaped or constructed [5]. Further, the material technology "vanishes from view in the preoccupation with the social" [14].

2.3 Social and Material Interaction Perspective

The third perspective is from a post-empiricist position that looks at how structure and agents are assumed to be interdependent systems that shape each other through ongoing interaction. This perspective has an ontological commitment to the dynamic interaction between structure and agency [15] and tends to adopt an interpretive approach [15]. However, other work that has adopted structuration in the context of technological change recognizes that technologies are constructed and reconstructed in their production and use, but that this process of social construction needs to account for the affordances associated with technology's physical properties [9, 11].

The main criticisms of this approach are that it assumes a duality and a separation between technology and social factors [15], that sometimes there is an emphasis on social over technological factors [8], and that another duality sometimes emerged, where "technologies became phenomena that existed in the 'realm of structure' while technology use existed in the 'realm of action'" [8]. This manifests as a tension between a form of soft technological determinism [8] and social practices [15].

2.4 Sociomaterial Assemblages Perspective

The fourth perspective is from an agential realist position that looks at how actors and objects, the social and the material, are constitutively entangled and analytically inseparable [14]. This perspective has an ontological commitment to the inherent inseparability of the sociomaterial assemblage and focuses on methodologies that can help to reveal the performativity of practice [15]. It has its roots in actor-network theory [7], relational ontology [4, 15], and phenomenologically-grounded research [19]. A sociomaterial perspective grounded in agential realism attempts to overcome the issues associated with perspectives that view the social and the material as distinct [13].

The main criticisms of this perspective are that it is conceptually vague, that the focus on performativity of practices ignores issues of power, role, and structure in organizations, and that it leaves out certain characteristics of organization that are important [13]. Further, while this perspective can describe a particular practice at a particular time, it is seen to have issues describing how practices are sustained and changed over time [8]. This perspective also treats all relations as mutually constitutive or co-dependent, which conceptualizes the social and the material as internally related, though in some cases these entities may be related, but in an external way, where the one does not need the other in order to exist [8].

2.5 Sociomaterial Imbrication Perspective

The fifth perspective is from a critical realist position that looks at how actors and objects, the social and the material, can be imbricated over time, while nevertheless retaining an analytical dualism [8, 13]. This perspective has an ontological commitment to sociomaterial agencies and focuses on methodologies that can look at both the realm of structure and the realm of action [8]. It takes the view that: "What the technology is does not change across space and time, but what it does can and often changes" [8]. It has its roots in Archer's 'morphogenetic' idea that structure predates action, but that structural elaboration postdates action [1]. A sociomaterial imbrication perspective grounded in critical realism attempts to overcome the issues associated with sociomateriality grounded in agential realism and provide a platform for the study of how sociomaterial phenomena are reconfigured over time.

The main criticism of this approach is that it represents an essentialist and dualistic worldview, though it would argue that this is purely analytical [3]. Further, assumptions about the value of studying changes in the relationships between analytically distinct material and social agency over time could be perceived to discredit the value of research that looks into practice-based phenomena at a given point in time [3].

2.6 Comparison of Perspectives

The following table compares the five theoretical perspectives described above (Table 1). It focuses on the characteristics of each approach rather than their guiding questions and conceptual contributions, which will be discussed and presented at the end of the following section on examples of these perspectives in use.

Table 1. Comparison of the five included theoretical perspectives

	Techno-centric	Human-centred	Social and material interaction	Sociomaterial assemblages	Sociomaterial imbrication
Ontology	Material and social are distinct	Material and social are distinct	Material and social are distinct	There is only the fusion of the social and material in the sociomaterial	Material and social are distinct, but become imbricated
Epistemology	Technology determines social and organizational characteristics	Social factors shape technology	The social and material are interdependent systems that shape each other through ongoing interaction	There is only a sociomaterial whole (though arbitrary agential cuts are sometimes needed for analysis)	Separate social and material elements become imbricated and reconfigure over time
Materiality	Material features of technology	Social construction of technology	Material features of technology that persist across place and time and that structure action	There is only the sociomaterial	Material features of technology that persist across place and time
Social	Social and organizational features	Social agency	Social agency	There is only the sociomaterial	Imbricated social and material agency
Unit of Analysis	Technological change	Relevant social groups surrounding technological development	Interaction between interpersonal communication, technology, and structure	Sociomaterial practice at a given time	Sociomaterial agencies over time

3   Examples of Foundational Theoretical Perspectives in Use

In this section, examples are provided to illustrate these five different perspectives and how they can be operationalized in practice to elucidate different aspects of the relationships between technology and social innovation. These examples help to demonstrate how each perspective may be appropriate under different circumstances in order to address different types of questions. This section is intended to motivate diversity in the theoretical foundations for different types of research and encourage researchers to be explicit about how their foundational theoretical perspectives guide their decisions and help shape their unique contributions to knowledge.

3.1   Sources of the Examples

The examples used in this section are drawn from the study of the design, development, implementation, adaptation, and use of technologies in public sector child protection services. While the focus on examples from a particular social service sector may not offer a breadth of different use cases, it helps to illustrate how a diverse set of theoretical foundations can be used to design research that can tackle different questions about social innovation within the same sector. These examples are a subset of the potential research designs and questions that can be adopted under each theoretical foundation, but they provide some guidance on the unique affordances of each perspective, which will be presented in a table at the end of this section.

The five examples illustrate each of the five foundational theoretical perspectives. The first is a survey of social workers that looks at the impact of a technological change on social worker perceptions about administrative burden [18]. The second looks at the influence of two relevant social groups, social workers and information and communication technology (ICT) professionals, on the development of an effective case management information system in Australia [20]. The third looks at how the social and material can interact to produce changes in the characteristics of information technology over time that allows for re-prioritization in the privileged forms of knowledge within the information system [17, 22]. The fourth looks at the challenges experienced by social workers from a technology-in-practice perspective when new structured decision making and integrated case management tools that are focused more on accountability and compliance were introduced [2]. The fifth looks at electronic documentation from a historical perspective and the resulting novel interface that was developed to handle a heterogeneous bundle of documents that make up the social care record [23].

3.2   Techno-Centric Example

A techno-centric perspective can provide insights into how technology is influencing organizational and social factors. In a period of technological change, a survey of 2,200 social care professionals in the UK found that more than half said that they spent more than 60% of their time on administrative work as opposed to direct client contact, while more than one-fifth spent over 80% of their time on such tasks, and 95% felt 'that social work had become more bureaucratic and less client-focussed over the previous five years' [18]. Here quantitative methods provided insights into the impact of technological changes on the degree of administrative burden in social work, highlighting how social innovation does not always follow technological change.

While this particular study does not provide details about the specific change that led to a concern by social workers about a shift from direct service to administrative requirements, it does provide some insights into the unintended impacts of technological change and the need for greater depth of understanding when trying to accomplish technologically supported social innovation. Techno-centric approaches can uncover high-level relationships between technological change and individual or organizational level outcomes, but it may not be able to reveal the details of that relationship. It may be able to reveal whether or not social innovation is taking place, but not why.

3.3 Human-Centred Example

A human-centred perspective can provide insights into how technology is shaped by organizational and social factors. In the context of the development of an ICT solution in Australia, a study looking at the involvement of relevant social groups, including social workers and ICT professionals, finds that socially shaped technology has realized greater successes in adoption and use than similar technologies in other jurisdictions, which had a compliance focus and lacked user-friendliness [20]. This Australian study took a social constructionist view of technological adoption indicating that there was a close relationship between social workers and IT professionals. Its findings indicated that: "The development of ICT programs for child welfare is a long-term and intensive process requiring the use of extensive resources to understand the social setting for both the underlying social work knowledge and computerization. Extensive resources and skills have been needed to marry both technologies with the service system culture" [20]. Here qualitative methods provided insights into socially innovative design and how the involvement of relevant social groups in this design and development could lead to more successful information technology adoption.

While this study does not provide details about the material characteristics of the technology, nor the experience of the technology in practice, it does provide insights into the social conditions under which successful information technologies can emerge. This type of research grounded in social constructivism can provide insights into the social conditions under which social innovation in child welfare case management system design, development, adoption, and use can be successful.

3.4 Social and Material Interaction Example

A social and material interaction perspective can be effective in providing insights into how material features of technology can structure how social work is done and, in turn, how social work can restructure technology to rebalance what knowledge is privileged within an information system. In the context of the forms of knowledge privileged by new information systems in Canada and the UK, qualitative studies looking at the forms of knowledge built into the structure of information systems find that the privileged forms of knowledge can potentially evolve as social groups take actions to restructure the information systems to meet their work-related needs [17, 22]. Here historical analysis and an interpretive approach were used to provide insights into how information technology could structure what knowledge was privileged and how changes to the technology could restructure the privileged forms of knowledge, in this case from knowledge focused on administrative compliance towards knowledge needed for holistic service delivery. Such knowledge was supported by basic data presentation tools, like dynamic genograms, that were commonly used in the sector prior to technological change and that helped support service provision.

While these studies look at structure embedded in information technology and the possibility of a restructuring based on social action, they do not look at the technologies in practice. They can provide insights into a process of interaction between structure and action over time. In particular, these studies can reveal how earlier structures that may look like failed attempts at social innovation can act as the foundation for either basic or socially innovative restructuring through social action.

3.5 Sociomaterial Assemblages Example

A sociomaterial assemblage perspective can be effective in providing insights into how technologies-in-practice are performed within organizations. In the context of new structured decision-making tools within a new integrated case management system in Queensland, Australia, and a new centralized case management system in Ontario, Canada, observing the technology in practice revealed failures in design and use, primarily related to a focus on compliance, performance reporting, and accountability, rather than to case management and direct service delivery [2, 21]. For example, there were "the attempts of practitioners to 'recode' the experiences and situations of children and parents to fit with the structures in the [integrated case management system] and the [structured decision-making] tools" [2]. These studies look at how the performance of the technology-in-practice assemblage allows for a combined focus on the material constraints on how information is collected, and the ways that workers found to resist, exert their agency, and record the information they need, even if this resulted in challenges for other information users in the service system. Here ethnomethodological and phenomenological approaches were used to provide insights into how the material and the social were constitutively entangled through the technologies-in-practice.

While these studies do not provide insights into external relations, nor changes in the technological and social assemblage over time, they do provide insights into how technologies that may be perceived to support social innovation, may not achieve that social innovation in practice. They also provide insights into ground-level sociomaterial innovation in response to top-down attempts at social innovation.

3.6 Sociomaterial Imbrication Example

A sociomaterial imbrication perspective provides insights into how material and social agencies become imbricated over time. In the context of the failed Integrated Children's System in the UK, which "shows the limitations of a management regime based on standardisation, targets and command-and-control" [23], a study finds that subsequent workshops to develop an effective virtual workspace prototype, which involved social workers in user-centred design, demonstrates the benefits of a sociomaterial imbrication perspective when seeking to understand the progress of technology supported social innovation over time [23]. This study focuses on how user-centred design offers an alternative design logic for socially innovative technology projects. Here an action research approach that included workshops and a prototype tool was used to provide insights into how the preceding material reality of the failed Integrated Children's System impacted social action and how the imbrication of the social and material could be reconfigured in attempts to progress the structural elaboration of a new system.

While this study does not provide details about the technologies in practice, it does provide insights into the imbrication of the social and the material and how material agency that precedes action can be the subject of subsequent structural elaboration, which could lead to progress in social innovation. It demonstrates how the imbrication and reconfiguration of the social and the material over time can lead to sociomaterial innovation, where technology is an inseparable element in the generation and implementation of new ideas about social relationships and social organization.

3.7 Comparison of Contributions Across Examples

The following table summarizes the guiding questions and potential contributions that each of the five perspectives offer (Table 2). This allows for a determination of which theoretical foundation to adopt depending on the objectives of research into social innovation.

Table 2. Comparison of contributions across the five included approaches

	Techno-centric	Human-centred	Social and material interaction	Sociomaterial assemblage	Sociomaterial imbrication
Question	How does technological change influence social innovation?	How does the social shaping of a technology influence social innovation?	How does the interaction between the social and the material influence social innovation?	What can sociomaterial practice tell us about social innovation?	What can the imbrication of social and material agency tell us about the progress of social innovation over time?
Contribution	The impact of technological change on social or organizational factors	The influence of relevant social groups on the shape of technologies	The interaction between structure embedded in technology and action over time	The performative aspects of technology-in-practice	The imbrication of the social and the material, such that what technology does can change across time

4 Discussion

This paper illustrates how the existing foundational theoretical perspectives for research into the study of social and material elements of technological change in organizational settings do not need to conflict, but instead can be adopted relative to different research questions and research design strategies.

This paper began by setting out the five perspectives on the theoretical foundations for the study of social and material phenomena in organizations. It specifically looked at techno-centric, human-centred, social and material interaction, sociomaterial assemblage, and sociomaterial imbrication perspectives, the unique characteristics of each, and their relationships. It then provided a set of examples in the child protection service sector to illustrate how each foundation could help to elucidate a different element of the material and social features of social innovation in the context of technological change. In particular, the example of social worker perspectives on changes in the sector towards a greater administrative focus, helps illustrate how a techno-centric approach can demonstrate the impact of technological change on social or organizational factors. The example of the development of a successful ICT system in Australia helps illustrate the influence of relevant social groups on the shape of technologies. The example of changes in the forms of knowledge structured within different information systems shows the interaction between structure embedded in technology and action over time. The example of structured decision-making and integrated case management tools in Queensland and Ontario, shows the performative aspects of technology-in-practice. The example of the workshops and prototype document management systems in the UK illustrates the promise of the imbrication of the social and the material, such that the way that technology becomes part of social agency can change over time.

Across all of the theoretical foundations it is possible to understand whether something is socially innovative, a failure of social innovation, or is merely the basics. The examples help to illustrate this by showing how, due to the different frames of reference that they prioritize, each of these perspectives can reveal different underlying factors for the success or failure of social innovation. For example, the case of social involvement of relevant social groups in the development of an ICT project in Australia shows an instance of social innovation success, through the long-term and intensive involvement of developers and users in contextually sensitive design. The case of social care professionals' opinions about a technological change indicates a failure in social innovation. Finally, the case of privileged forms of knowledge in Canada and the UK shows how applying basic technological fixes is really just something that should have been done initially. The public sector is unique and the simple transplantation of private sector innovation is not sufficient. Instead, social innovation comes from tailoring existing innovations to the public sector context. Understanding the different but complementary reasons why or why not involves using more than one perspective. The theoretical perspectives that focus on interaction, practice, and imbrication over time, may serve to illustrate how simply adopting what is in the private sector is not innovative, but that taking technologies or design, implementation, and organizational change strategies that are tried and tested and adapting them for a public sector setting is more appropriately the place where we can hope to identify instances of social innovation.

5 Conclusion

The illustration of different perspectives on the theoretical foundations for the study of technology in social settings such as public sector organizations, can provide insights into the applicability of each foundation to various questions about social innovation. They can also help to reveal different types of factors that can influence social innovation (for example, the materiality of technology, the social reality, the combination of these two, the idiosyncrasies of practices, or sociomaterial change over time). This analysis of the foundational theoretical perspectives also suggests that we should not only think in terms of social innovation, but in terms of sociomaterial innovation, where the social and material, people and technologies, are inextricably linked [6]. The hope is that the examples and summaries provided here can help researchers of social innovation in the public sector to make informed decisions about the theoretical foundations upon which they choose to build their research questions and designs. Through the adoption of these different perspectives, researchers will be better equipped to identify what constitutes #innobasics, what characterizes failures in social innovation, and where social innovation actually occurs.

Acknowledgements. This research was supported by the Clarendon Fund and the Social Sciences and Humanities Research Council of Canada, Doctoral Fellowship number 752-2017-0529. Research ethics approval was received from the University of Oxford with reference number SSH OII C1A 18 055.

References

1. Archer, M.S.: Realist Social Theory: The Morphogenetic Approach. Cambridge University Press, Cambridge (1995)
2. Gillingham, P.: The development of electronic information systems for the future: practitioners, 'embodied structures' and 'technologies-in-practice'. Br. J. Soc. Work **43**(3), 430–445 (2012). https://doi.org/10.1093/bjsw/bcr202
3. Hultin, L.: On becoming a sociomaterial researcher: exploring epistemological practices grounded in a relational, performative ontology. Inf. Organ. **29**(2), 91–104 (2019). https://doi.org/10.1016/j.infoandorg.2019.04.004
4. Kallinikos, J.: The Consequences of Information: Institutional Implications of Technological Change. Elgar, Cheltenham (2006)
5. Klein, H.K., Kleinman, D.L.: The social construction of technology: structural considerations. Sci. Technol. Hum. Values **27**(1), 28–52 (2002). https://doi.org/10.1177/016224390 202700102
6. Klischewski, R.: Will the government machine turn into a monster? In: Proceedings of the 20th Annual International Conference on Digital Government Research, United Arab Emirates, Dubai, pp. 306–313 (2019)
7. Latour, B.: Reassembling the Social: An Introduction to Actor-Network-Theory. OUP, Oxford (2005)
8. Leonardi, P.M.: Theoretical foundations for the study of sociomateriality. Inf. Organ. **23**(2), 59–76 (2013). https://doi.org/10.1016/j.infoandorg.2013.02.002
9. Leonardi, P.M.: When flexible routines meet flexible technologies: affordance, constraint, and the imbrication of human and material agencies. MIS Q. **35**(1), 147–167 (2011). https://doi.org/10.2307/23043493

10. Leonardi, P.M., Barley, S.R.: What's under construction here? Social action, materiality, and power in constructivist studies of technology and organizing. Acad. Manage. Ann. **4**(1), 1–51 (2010). https://doi.org/10.5465/19416521003654160

11. Luna-Reyes, L.F., Zhang, J., Ramón Gil-García, J., Cresswell, A.M.: Information systems development as emergent socio-technical change: a practice approach. Eur. J. Inf. Syst. **14**(1), 93–105 (2005). https://doi.org/10.1057/palgrave.ejis.3000524

12. MacKenzie, D.A., Wajcman, J.: The Social Shaping of Technology. Open University Press, London (1999)

13. Mutch, A.: Sociomateriality—taking the wrong turning? Inf. Organ. **23**(1), 28–40 (2013). https://doi.org/10.1016/j.infoandorg.2013.02.001

14. Orlikowski, W.J.: Sociomaterial practices: exploring technology at work. Organ. Stud. **28**(9), 1435–1448 (2007). https://doi.org/10.1177/0170840607081138

15. Orlikowski, W.J., Scott, S.V.: Sociomateriality: challenging the separation of technology, work and organization. Acad. Manage. Ann. **2**(1), 433–474 (2008). https://doi.org/10.1080/19416520802211644

16. Pahlka, J.: The CIO Problem, Part 2: Innovation. Code for America, San Francisco (2016)

17. Parton, N.: Changes in the form of knowledge in social work: from the 'social' to the 'informational'? Br. J. Soc. Work **38**(2), 253–269 (2006)

18. Samuel, M.: Social care professionals overwhelmed by paperwork. Commun. Care. **14**(December), 8 (2005)

19. Suchman, L.A.: Human-Machine Reconfigurations Plans and Situated Actions. Cambridge University Press, Cambridge (2007)

20. Tregeagle, S.: Heads in the cloud: an example of practice-based information and communication technology in child welfare. J. Technol. Hum. Serv. **34**(2), 224–239 (2016). https://doi.org/10.1080/15228835.2016.1177479

21. Vogl, T.M.: Artificial intelligence and organizational memory in government: the experience of record duplication in the child welfare sector in Canada. In: Proceedings of dg.o 2020, Seoul, South Korea, June 2020 (2020)

22. Vogl, T.M.: The impact of information technology evolution on the forms of knowledge in public sector social work: examples from Canada and the UK. In: Proceedings of the 53rd Hawaii International Conference on System Sciences, Maui, Hawaii, USA (2020)

23. Wastell, D., White, S.: Making sense of complex electronic records: socio-technical design in social care. Appl. Ergon. **45**(2), Part A, 143–149 (2014). https://doi.org/10.1016/j.apergo.2013.02.002. Advances in Socio-Technical Systems Understanding and Design: A Festschrift in Honour of K.D. Eason

Open Government and Transparency

Digital Transformation in the Context of the Open Government Partnership

Noella Edelmann[1]($\boxtimes$) (iD) and Mary Francoli[2] (iD)

[1] Danube University, Krems, Austria
Noella.Edelmann@donau-uni.ac.at
[2] Carleton University, Ottawa, ON, Canada
mary.francoli@carleton.ca

Abstract. This paper explores the connection between membership in the Open Government Partnership (OGP) and digital transformation. It employs a qualitative research approach and document analysis to examine OGP Independent Reporting Mechanism (IRM) Reports and government self-assessment reports, to get a sense of the nature of digital transformation commitments made within OGP national action plans. This includes a look at what the commitments are, why they are made, and their results. Ultimately, it is found that while few OGP members focus on achieving digital transformation results, most are not leveraging their membership to advance digital transformation. Moreover, those that do are not doing so in a way that addresses a clear policy or governance issue, rendering it difficult to comment on whether the commitments are effectively advancing open government. The mandatory assessment of OGP action plans helps, to some degree, to drive members to complete their commitments, and serves as a useful tool for advancing policies as they relate to open government.

Keywords: Digital transformation · Open Government Partnership · Qualitative research

1 Introduction

Today, we are witnessing important connections between digital technology and governance, particularly within the open government movement. Governments joining the Open Government Partnership (OGP), for example, all sign the Open Government Declaration in which they commit to, among other things, using digital technology to advance improved governance: "We commit to developing accessible and secure online spaces as platforms for delivering services, engaging the public, and sharing information and ideas." [1]. In this way, OGP membership, can be viewed, in part, as a platform for advancing digital transformation.

The goal of this paper is to understand how digital transformation is understood in the context of the OGP. It asks: (1) How is digital transformation understood in countries that have membership in OGP? And (2) how does membership in OGP facilitate

S. Hofmann et al. (Eds.): ePart 2020, LNCS 12220, pp. 69–80, 2020.
https://doi.org/10.1007/978-3-030-58141-1_6

the implementation of digital transformation strategies? To answer these questions, a qualitative research design based on document analysis was used to analyse OGP action plans and assessment documents according to a definition of digital transformation by Mergel et al. [2] in the public sector that considers several dimensions: the objects that are to be digitally transformed, the reasons to do so, the processes and the results to be achieved. This study shows that not only are few countries with OGP membership using their membership to digitally transform the public sector, it also reveals that they focus on digital transformation mainly in terms of the results to be achieved. This paper starts by looking at literature on digital transformation and open government. This is followed by a discussion on research design, results, analysis and discussion.

2   Literature Review

Digital technology has spurred organizations across all sectors to develop strategies to harness the benefits that digitalization brings to manufacturing, service delivery, customer relations, and human resource development. Strategies will usually involve the explicit transformation of key business operations to impact product development, internal and external workflow processes, organizational structures, but also company values and concepts. All digital transformation strategies have four central dimensions: the technologies used in an organisation, the attitudes towards them and their adoption, the expected and actual impact of digital technology strategies on value chains, changes in organizational structure by incorporating digital technologies and activities, and the financial aspects driving transformation [3]. Before developing a digital strategy, it is important to know what digital transformation is, Mergel et al. [2], for example define it as "*a comprehensive organizational approach*" that does not have a "*measurable and defined end status, as well as a fixed budget. Instead, digital transformation is a continuous process that needs frequent adjustments of its processes, services, and products to external needs*" (p. 10).

Similarly, governments and public administrations aim to transform internal workflow processes, modes of service delivery, and channels of communication with their stakeholders using digital technologies. The emergence and proliferation of digital tools and the digital transformation of public organizations has led to several initiatives, reforms and new principles, and policies. The Tallinn Declaration [4] is one example of a non-binding agreement encouraging governments to provide digital services that are seamless, secure, open, transparent and interoperable. Thus, government's use of information technology is to create public value by achieving organizational change, improving service delivery, understanding users' needs [5] and to make changes to institutional structures and arrangements that may lead to a reduction of costs, the development of (better) policies, increasing efficiency and effectivity [6]. Digital tools can also be employed to sustain multiple or changing public values, support collaboration between the stakeholders, ensure public accountability by increasing transparency and openness [7]. This sort of proactive and digital disclosure is at the heart of contemporary open government. Open, transparent, and accountable government represents the basis of an informed citizenry and advances in social media, data analytics, coding, citizen engagement approaches, open and big data, and citizens' demands all lead to an unprecedented open government that is increasingly ongoing, interactive and transparent [8]. Openness requires that governments establish a range of approaches, processes, infrastructure, and policies to ensure that citizens, civil society, and others have access to government information, data, and participatory mechanisms today and in future.

Open government is intimately linked to other concepts that are at the intersection of technology and governance, including e-government [9, 10] and government 2.0 [11]. However, open government is broader. It represents the capacity of new technologies and a fundamental shift in the culture and practice of governance that extends beyond the web 2.0 platform on which government 2.0 is based. As Don Tapscott states, it is a "redesign of how government operates; how and what the public sector provides and ultimately how governments interact and engage with their citizens" [11 p. xvi]. This redesign does not mean a radical or sudden departure from previous modes of operation; rather, we might think of it as the maturation of e-government and government 2.0. Its emphasis is on sharing, the distribution of power and collaboration. It includes things such as peoples' right to access documents and government proceedings, meaningful participation of citizens and better communication between branches and levels of government [12].

One of the most notable drivers of open government for almost a decade has been the Open Government Partnership (OGP). Founded in 2011 by eight national governments, membership now includes 78 national governments and 20 local governments [13]. It brings together governments and civil society in an effort to develop and implement strategies to foster "accountable, responsive, and inclusive governance" [14]. Members must sign the *Open Government Declaration* [1], which sets out a number of shared values and commitments, including a commitment to harness digital technology. In addition, government members are obligated to co-create, with civil society, national action plans (NAP) every two years. The plans outline a series of commitments to be implemented over the two-year life cycle of the NAP that will improve open government. In this way, NAPs can serve as one important platform for moving specific agendas or policies, such as digital transformation, forward. OGP membership also requires agreeing to have NAPs and progress toward completion is assessed by an Independent Reporting Mechanism (IRM). The IRM process, as it relates specifically to national members, has changed considerably since the start of OGP resulting in different types of reports.

While all members are assessed by IRM, many also followed OGP processes, which have also changed over time, and delivered their own self-assessment at the mid and end of terms milestones of their NAPs. As will be discussed below, all of the IRM and self-assessment documents are useful to understanding government priorities, and actions. In the case of this paper, and as will be discussed further in the research design section that follows, the NAP and these assessment documents allow us to see what governments are focusing on when it comes to digital transformation, as well as how it has been moved forward, if at all.

3   Research Design and Methodology

For this study, the researchers aim to understand how those countries that have membership in the OGP understand and implement digital transformation. A qualitative approach was selected for this study as qualitative research promotes a deep understanding of real-world complexity and can lead to an in-depth description and explanation of what is being investigated [15]. This study is therefore an exploratory study and document analysis was used to gain the data needed to answer the research questions. Given that understanding is the primary goal, the researchers are central to both data collection and analysis. The results thus represent a rich description of the phenomena [16] rather than "objective" post-positivist answers.

In order to answer the research questions, documentary analysis was used to gather information from selected texts and to study the content according the relevant dimensions. To investigate the extent to which countries with OGP membership understand and implement digital transformation, the documents used for analysis were systematically selected. It is important to consider the documents selected for and to assess their authenticity in order to explore their content [17]. The analysis of the documents is based on a process of "evaluating documents in such a way that empirical knowledge is produced and understanding is developed" [18 p. 33].

Krippendorf [19] suggests that documents or other text data such as government guidelines and directives, official documents, programs and policies and periodic reports can be analysed in a hermeneutic approach through a five-step process including: (1) access to documents and data, (2) checking the validity of documents, (3) comprehending the documents, (4) analysing the data, and (5) applying the information to themes. Using these principles, the documents identified in the electronic database were screened for validity and checked for comprehensibility, then analysed. After identifying the relevant commitments, the researchers were able to undertake documentary research by looking at the membership pages [13] for the four countries with relevant commitments. From each member's page, it was possible to locate relevant IRM reports, as well as any government self-assessments done related to the commitments in question.

Bowen recommends that a document review should lead to the identification of meaningful and relevant passages of text or other data rather than engaging in a numeric quantification [18]. The researchers therefore decided to consider and analyse all the documents according to the coding structure developed in Mergel et al. [2]. They considered and analysed all the documents according to the codes of the following themes: what is the focus of digital transformation (the "object"), how will digital transformation occur (the "process"), why is needs to occur (the "reason") and what results are expected (the "results") [2]. Thus, on the one hand, the coding leads to numeric results, at the same time, analysing the coded material allows the qualitative analysis of the results.

3.1 Document Analysis

The document began with the identification of the commitments made within OGP NAPs that relate to digital transformation. To do this, the researchers used the OGP Explorer, a database of 3856 commitments made within OGP NAPs from 2011 to 2018 [20]. Ultimately, only 7 of 3856 commitments contained a reference to digital transformation (data regarding the relevant commitments are valid as of March 22, 2020 when search was conducted). These included: 1 commitment from Australia, 4 from France, 1 from Italy, and 1 from Sweden. While this paper focuses on trends and attitudes toward digital transformation, more generally, and less on the specific of each commitment, it is useful to note the focus of each of the seven commitments. The full text of each commitment can be found in the relevant NAPs cited in Table 1:

Table 1. OGP commitments analysed

Country	NAP	Commitment title
Australia	2016–18 [21]	Digitally transform the delivery of government services
France	2018–20 [22]	Developing an open science ecosystem
"	"	Increasing transparency in public procurement
"	"	Organize an international GovTech summit in France
"	2015–17 [23]	Grow a Culture of Openness Data Literacy and Digital Technologies
Italy	2016–18 [24]	Lecce Start up in the City
Sweden	2016–18 [25]	Putting citizens at the centre eGovernment of government administration reforms

The document selection process led to the identification of 10 documents from 4 countries to be analysed. They represented either a government self-assessment (N = 3) or an Independent Reporting Mechanism (IRM) assessment (N = 7). It should be noted that the distribution of the available reports was not consistent across the four countries. Italy, for example, did not have a government self-assessment. Similarly, there was only one available IRM report for Australia, whereas France has four (remembering it has multiple commitments related to digital transformation), and Italy and Sweden each have two.

Government self-assessments are created by OGP member countries and provide varying levels of detail on progress made toward completion of commitments. Some have offered mid-term and end-of-term reports while others might offer one or the other, and others still will not undertake the assessment. These reports are useful as they can clarify the goal of the commitment, the rationale for including it in country's NAP, progress toward completion, along with mention of issues that might be helping or hindering completion.

While the IRM reports contain some of the same information, it originates from a different source that is supposed to be both neutral, and independent of government [26]. In general, the IRM reports on adherence to the OGP process, the quality of co-creation activities, the fit of NAP commitments to the open government context in the country being assessed (does the NAP help to solve some of the challenges to open government in the country), and completion levels of commitments. The IRM reports also make recommendations to government on how, and whether, to move forward with commitments. The reports themselves generate a lot of data and are useful for getting an overview of open government activities within individual member countries, and across OGP.

4 Results

All the available government self-assessments [21–25] and IRM reports [27–33] were coded by one researcher only according to the dimensions in Mergel et al. [2]: (1) the focus of digital transformation (the "object"), (2) how will digital transformation occur (the "process"), (3) reasons for its transformation (the "reasons"), and (4) results are expected (the "results") [2]. Nvivo was used to upload, analyse and code the documents and to extract the results.[1]

The coding showed that the documents focus on the results and to a lesser extent, processes and objects of digital transformation, whilst the reasons were hardly mentioned.

4.1 Government Self-assessments

On the basis of the 4 dimensions coded, the government self-assessments [21–25] focus on "results" to be gained through digital transformation (72.73%) and to a lesser extent, the "process" of digital transformation (18.18%). The "object" that is to be digitally transformed is hardly mentioned, the reasons for requiring digital transformation not at all (0%).

4.2 Independent Reporting Mechanism (IRM)

The main focus of all the IRM reports [27–33] was on the "results" (57%), whilst the "object" (21%) and "process" of digital transformation played smaller roles. The "reasons" for digital transformation were close to 0. This breakdown is perhaps unsurprising given that one of the primary goals of the IRM reports is to provide an overview of completion and results.

5 Analysis

In the analysis, the 4 dimensions of digital transformation and the main focus of each country within the OGP documents referring to digital transformation is analysed in greater depth. Whilst all countries focused on the results to be achieved, France also considers the process of digital transformation and Italy the objects to be transformed. The analysis is presented by country, in order to show to the similarities and differences between the only 4 countries with OGP membership which mention "digital transformation" in commitments contained in the OGP Explorer.

---

[1] Note: Due to space limitations the authors were not able to include the code book and full findings here, but will happily provide it via email to those interested.

5.1 Australia

The GSA and the IRM documents analysed show that Australia focuses on the results or outcomes to be achieved (74%), more than the process (14%) or the outcomes of digital transformation (11%). The reasons were not considered.

Thus, the GSA focuses on achieving results such as better interactions: *"make government services simpler, faster and cheaper. Better services will make it easier for the public to work and interact with Government"* and by developing the necessary digital environment: *"government agencies and departments now have a platform for reporting their service performance publicly, and a framework for measuring user satisfaction"* [27]. The Australian IRM mid-term report also focuses on results in terms of better interactions: *"The Digital Service Standard applies to all new, redesigned or high volume transactional services, allowing individuals and business to transact with the government, including providing information, money or goods, or new or redesigned services providing information to the public"* by using a digital environment (*"Digital Marketplace"*) although there is some is some concern in the IRM *"that it was not being widely promoted, particularly in sectors not traditionally involved with government software and hardware procurement"* [28]. The role of policies as an outcome is particularly important for both types of documents (25%) [21, 27, 28]. Both point out the necessity to prepare a digital transformation roadmap understood as a "Digital Transformation Map" and "Individual Sector Maps" [21]. This necessity is reflected in the Mid-Term IRM report as a *"whole-of-government digital transformation roadmap"* as well as *"agency-level digital transformation roadmaps"* and *"sector-specific roadmaps,"* but also a *"Digital Transformation Office"* and the role of *"the National Archives of Australia and the Office of the Australian Information Commissioner (…) to assist agencies in developing their digital delivery systems while developing common platforms and standard"* [28]. The *"Agency or sector-specific roadmaps could be developed and continually reviewed by the DTA"* are seen as being important as the provide *"information to the public on the potential benefits of future developments"* [28]. The government self-assessment points out that the "Whole-of-Government Digital Transformation Map" was delivered in 2016, to be followed by the sector-wide strategies to follow [21].

5.2 France

The GSA [22] and the IRM documents [29, 33] show that the main focus is on the results of digital transformation (53%), to some extent the process (34%) and finally the object of digital transformation (10%). Only the 2015–17 IRM report [33] considers the reasons, but only to a minor extent (2%).

The government's ambition is not only to achieve a digital culture, such as to *"grow a culture of openness, data literacy and digital technologies"* [33], but also to showcase the country as a leading digital nation, that is to *"bring the GovTech ecosystem fully into the limelight by cementing France's position as a country of authority on the subject and by showcasing the success stories"* and *"to give France a position of influence in the tech field"* [29]. This is echoed in the processes required to achieve these results in open science commitment where *"the ministry of France's efforts to facilitate open access to scientific research constitutes part of a global initiative"* [29]. The reports are not always optimistic and show that there are still several issues regarding the processes that need to be addressed in order to achieve these results: "*an article (...) at Le Monde, claimed that even the political and social elite in France are overwhelmed by digital technology*" and the "*lack of public information regarding high-level activities concerning digital knowledge and training makes it difficult for the IRM researcher to gauge completion of this activity*" [33]. Not only the public, but the French government still needs to undertake certain efforts in order to achieve the results: "*we want the open government mindset to catch on, we need not only proactive efforts on the part of Government itself, but also support for the stakeholders.*" [29].

5.3 Italy

The results draw on a single IRM report [30] and focuses only on the objects to be digitally transformed (58.3%) and the results to be gained (41.6%).

In terms of the objects to be transformed, it is interesting to see that the documents addresses and encourages the private rather than the public sector: "*rewarding innovative start-ups and SMEs which meet the technological requirements of administrations and help solve their problems*" [30]. The results are also the outcome of the better relationships, more between the private and the public sector: "*to better connect start-ups and public administrations.*" than between citizens and the public sector "*While this commitment aimed to remove bureaucratic obstacles for companies and to gain from the expertise of start-ups and small and medium-size enterprises (SMEs) to the technological needs of institutions, it was not clearly relevant to the OGP values of access to information, citizen's ability to participate in decision-making, or public accountability*" [30].

5.4 Sweden

The Swedish reports [31, 32] focus mainly on results to be gained (60.1%), than the object (27%) or the process (13%). The reasons are not considered.

The government self-assessment notes that through digital transformation "*transparency and participation must increase*" and be able to "*contribute to the target of an increasingly open government that supports innovation and participation*" [31].

The mid-term IRM report sees the involvement of as an important result that is to be achieved: The Digital First programme is debated with stakeholders, and the Swedish council is committed to getting advice once a year "*from digital change leaders in civil society, and from businesses and citizens*" [32]. The government holds a public consultation about a "*new government body coordinating digital transformation efforts*" adding that the response gained shows" that the stakeholders consider this an important issue" [32], but the "*Ministry of Finance could make the next open council more result-oriented and involve potential developers, users, and the middle-management of the open of public agencies, as well as use more experimental hackathon methods (...) also clearly communicate to participants how the results of council will feed into the decision-making process*" [32]. The end of term IRM Report echoes many of the comments made in the mid-term report adding that "*public agencies in Sweden are generally advanced in digital public services,*" but that there is "*an increasing polarization among the less digitally*" *mature and more digitally mature agencies. The same is true among municipalities. One key challenge is to improve digital management and coordination"* [31].

6 Discussion and Conclusions

In closing, we return to our original research questions: (1) How is digital transformation understood in countries that have membership in OGP? And (2) how does membership in OGP facilitate the implementation of digital transformation strategies?

In regard to the first question, it is fair to say that digital transformation has not been a priority for OGP members, at least not in the context of open government. In this regard, the conclusion is that OGP membership is not being leveraged as a tool to advance digital transformation. This is evidenced by the small number of commitments identified in this paper focusing on digital transformation (7 out of 3856). It could be that OGP members, including those discussed in this paper, have digital transformation initiatives that are being conducted outside of the scope of OGP NAPs. Given the methodology used here, this would not be captured in the research conducted for this paper. This finding in itself is significant as it shows a sort of disconnect between open government and digital transformation in spite of the emphasis placed on digital technology within the Open Government Declaration signed by all OGP members. It signals a potential lost opportunity.

Within the few countries that do include commitments to digital transformation, the analysis offered in this paper shows that while they all focus on the results to be achieved, France also considers the process of digital transformation. In addition, Italy focuses on the objects to be transformed. This indicates that most of the other dimensions of digital transformation are not considered in particular depth by the majority of countries.

The findings also hint at a potential problem in the writing of OGP commitments. As is demonstrated by this small sample, few commitments talk about what should be transformed or why. Most simply state a desired result to be achieved. In this sense, there is some evidence to indicate that there is a potential disconnect between commitments in NAPs and the open government challenges in OGP member countries. NAPs are not as strategic, problem, or policy oriented as they could be to move forward ambitious change.

In regard to the second research question, it appears that membership in OGP helps members to implement their commitments. Overall, high levels of completion were achieved across the countries studied. This could, in part, mean that governments are particularly motived to implement commitments when they know that their success will be assessed and reported on. Thought of in this way, we can see that the OGP NAPs can be a useful mechanism for advancing goals and strategies related to digital transformation. This suggests that perhaps the linkage between OGP and digital transformation could be stronger moving forward for governments which wish to advance digital transformation to transform public administration in order to adapt to the changing environment and address societal challenges. Although management changes are underway, some visions of what digital government may achieve seem over-optimistic as they hope that bureaucracy will be banished or that the "virtual state" will be the outcome [34].

The researchers recognize that there are some limitations to the methodology used for this paper. The qualitative assessment used is built on documentary research including

IRM reports and government self-assessments. There are gaps in the reports in some countries. This reflects a difficultly in conducting research across OGP membership. Not all countries are on the same action plan cycle, the IRM process and reports have changed over time, and not all governments produce self-assessments. While this can be problematic, this paper aimed to get a high-level view of what was going on with digital transformation in each country. As such missing reports do not have a major impact on the overall conclusions. The impact is further minimized when noting that the IRM researchers gather much of the information used in their reports through interactions with government.

A more significant limitation is that the methodology used here does not readily allow much insight into the context for digital transformation in each country. To better understand this, future research could build upon this study to allow for broader documentary research, outside of the scope of OGP reporting, to get a more fulsome idea of progress made toward digital transformation in each of the countries studied here. Additionally, interviews with key government officials involved in implementing either OGP or digital transformation, would allow for a richer and more nuanced understanding of the trajectory of digital transformation, and how it could, or should, link to open government.

References

1. OGP: Open Government Declaration. https://www.opengovpartnership.org/process/joining-ogp/open-government-declaration/. Accessed 22 Mar 2020
2. Mergel, I., Edelmann, N., Haug, N.: Defining digital transformation: results from expert interviews. Gov. Inf. Q. 36(4), 101385 (2019)
3. Matt, C., Hess, T., Benlian, A.: Digital transformation strategies. J Bus. Inf. Syst. Eng. 57(5), 339–343 (2015)
4. Tallinn Declaration on eGovernment (2017). https://ec.europa.eu/digital-single-market/en/news/ministerial-declaration-egovernment-tallinn-declaration. Accessed 10 Mar 2020
5. Luna-Reyes, L.F., Gil-Garcia, J.R.: Digital government transformation and internet portals: the co-evolution of technology, organizations, and institutions. Gov. Inf. Q. 31(4), 545–555 (2014)
6. Weerakkody, V., Omar, A., El-Haddadeh, R., Al-Busaidy, M.: Digitally-enabled service transformation in the public sector: the lure of institutional pressure and strategic response towards change. Gov. Inf. Q. 33(4), 658–668 (2016)
7. Lindgren, I., van Veenstra, A.F.: Digital government transformation: a case illustrating public e-service development as part of public sector transformation. In: Janssen, M., Chun, S.A. (eds.) Proceedings of the 19th Annual International Conference on Digital Government Research: Governance in the Data Age, Delft, The Netherlands, pp. 1–6. ACM (2018)
8. Edelmann, N., Parycek, P., Krimmer, R., Buchsbaum, T., Pieber, L.: Eastern Partnership eDemocracy - Politics in the Digital Age. Danube University Krems, Krems, Austria, 23 October 2018 (2018). https://digitalgovernment.files.wordpress.com/2018/11/eap-edem-conference-2018-report_final_january-2019.pdf. Accessed 10 Mar 2020
9. Jaeger, P.T.: The endless wire: e-government as global phenomenon. Gov. Inf. Q. 4(20), 323–331 (2003)
10. Silcock, R.: What is e-government. Parliam. Aff. 54(1), 88–101 (2001)
11. Tapscott, D.: Foreword. In: Lathrop, D., Ruma, L. (eds.) Open Government: Collaboration, Transparency, and Participation in Practice. O'Reilly, Sebastopol (2010)

12. Lathrop, D., Ruma, L.: Open Government: Collaboration, Transparency, and Participation in Practice. O'Reilly Media Inc, Sebastopol (2010)
13. OGP: OGP   Members.   https://www.opengovpartnership.org/our-members/#national. Accessed 22 Mar 2020
14. About OGP. https://www.opengovpartnership.org/about/. Accessed 22 Mar 2020
15. Bloomberg, L., Volpe, M.: Completing Your Qualitative Dissertation: A Roadmap From Beginning to End (Forum Qualitative Sozialforschung/Forum: Qualitative Social Research). Sage, Los Angeles (2009)
16. Geertz, C.: The Interpretation of Cultures. Basic Books, New York (1973)
17. O'Leary, Z.: The Essential Guide to Doing Your Research Project. Sage, Thousand Oaks (2017)
18. Bowen, G.A.: Document analysis as a qualitative research method. Qual. Res. J. **9**(2), 27 (2009)
19. Krippendorff, K.: Content Analysis: An Introduction to Its Methodology. Sage publications, Thousand Oaks (2018)
20. OGP Explorer. https://www.opengovpartnership.org/tag/ogp-explorer/
21. Commonwealth of Australia Department of the Prime Minister and Cabinet: Australia's first Open Government National Action Plan 2016–2018. https://www.opengovpartnership.org/wp-content/uploads/2017/04/Australia_NAP_2016-2018_0.pdf. Accessed 22 Mar 2020
22. République Francaise: Pour une Action Publique Transparente et Collaborative: Plan d'Action National Pour la France 2018–2020. https://www.opengovpartnership.org/wp-content/upl oads/2018/04/France_Action-Plan_2018-2020.pdf. Accessed 22 Mar 2020
23. République Francaise Mission Etalab–Secretary-General for Government Modernization: For a Transparent and Collaborative Government: France National Action Plan 2015–2017. https://www.opengovpartnership.org/wp-content/uploads/2019/06/2015-07-09_Plan-gouvernement-ouvert-EN-Version-Finale_0.pdf. Accessed 22 Mar 2020
24. Government of Italy Ministro per la Semplificazione e la Pubblica Amministrazione: Open Government in Italy 3rd Action Plan with Addendum 2016–2018. https://www.opengovpa rtnership.org/wp-content/uploads/2017/06/Italy_NAP3_2016-18_EN_revised.pdf. Accessed 22 Mar 2020
25. Government of Sweden: Sweden's Third National Action Plan for Open Government Partnership 2016–2018. https://www.opengovpartnership.org/wp-content/uploads/2019/06/Swe den_National-Action-Plan-3_2016-18.pdf. Accessed 22 Mar 2020
26. About the IRM. https://www.opengovpartnership.org/process/accountability/about-the-irm/. Accessed 22 Mar 2020
27. Department of the Prime Minister and Cabinet (Australia): Australia End of Term Self-Assessment 2016–2018. https://www.opengovpartnership.org/wp-content/uploads/2019/03/Australia_End-Term_Self-Assessment_2016-2018.pdf. Accessed 22 Mar 2020
28. Stewart, D.: Australia IRM Mid Term Report 2016–2018. Australian National University. https://www.opengovpartnership.org/wp-content/uploads/2018/05/Australia_Mid-Term_R eport_2016-2018.pdf. Accessed 22 Mar 2020
29. Wickberg, S.: France IRM Design Report 2018–2020. Sciences Po. https://www.opengo vpartnership.org/wp-content/uploads/2019/11/France_Design_Report_2018-2020_EN.pdf. Accessed 22 Mar 2020
30. Segato, L., Capello, N.: Italy IRM End of Term Report 2016–18. https://www.opengovpartn ership.org/documents/italy-end-of-term-report-2016-2018/. Accessed 22 Mar 2020
31. N.N.: Sweden End of Term Self-Assessment Report 2016–18. https://www.opengovpartners hip.org/wp-content/uploads/2018/12/Sweden_End-Term_Self-Assessment_2016-2018.pdf. Accessed 22 Mar 2020

32. Ostling, A.: Sweden Mid Term IRM Report 2016–18. https://www.opengovpartnership.org/wp-content/uploads/2018/10/Sweden_Mid-Term_Report_2016-2018_EN.pdf. Accessed 22 Mar 2020

33. Wickberg, S.: France IRM End of Term Report 2015–2017. https://www.opengovpartnership.org/wp-content/uploads/2018/07/France_End-of-Term_Report_2015-2017.pdf. Accessed 22 Mar 2020

34. Dunleavy, P., Margetts, H., Bastow, S., Tinkler, J.: New public management is dead—long live digital-era governance. J. Public Adm. Res. Theor. 16(3), 467–494 (2006)

What to Be Disclosed? Attributes of Online Games for the Market Transparency Policy

Changwoo Suh[1], Byungtae Lee[1], Habin Lee[2(✉)], Youngseok Choi[3], and Sunghan Ryu[4]

[1] Korea Advanced Institute of Science and Technology, Seoul, South Korea
changwoo.suh@gmail.com, btlee@kaist.ac.kr
[2] Brunel University London, Uxbridge, UK
habin.lee@brunel.ac.uk
[3] University of Southampton, Southampton, UK
y.choi@soton.ac.uk
[4] Shanghai Jiao Tong University, Shanghai, China
shryu@sjtu.edu.cn

Abstract. This paper identifies main features of online games to be disclosed to the market for policy makers. It tests the positive relationships between information disclosure for online games and stock returns using event analysis method. Based on data collected from online game companies between 2004 to 2009 in South Korea, the paper finds positive and significant correlation between game rating information and stock reactions. Specifically, the positive reactions are clear when a company introduces casual games, and a company has development capability. However, we do not find any significant relationships between stock reactions and voluntary information releases after the game rating information released. The findings support the feasibility of introduction of mandatory information disclosure scheme for online game industry.

Keywords: Information disclosure · Online game · Information spillover · Stock returns

1 Introduction

Information disclosure is widely used by policy makers to protect public interests in many countries for protecting environment, ensuring health and preventing market failures in finance. FDA mandates drug companies to disclose the details of any new products to protect publics from any side effects. Mandatory disclosure of fuel mix percentages and pollution discharge statistics of electricity companies led to reduced use of fossil fuels and increased use of clean fuels in US (Delmas et al. 2010). It is reported that disclosure of financial information of companies leads to reduced liquidity, lower cost of capital, and more efficient market through reducing information asymmetry (Verrecchia 2004). Recently, scholars and policy makers are designing biodiversity index for

© IFIP International Federation for Information Processing 2020
Published by Springer Nature Switzerland AG 2020
S. Hofmann et al. (Eds.): ePart 2020, LNCS 12220, pp. 81–92, 2020.
https://doi.org/10.1007/978-3-030-58141-1_7

companies to enforce companies disclose how their business activities making impact on the biodiversity in the ecosystem (Skouloudis et al. 2019).

As online games are forming an important industry over the world, policy makers are pressed to control the market in particular for transparency issues. The policy makers are in black on what information is required to be disclosed to provide right information for investors due to the new and unique nature of the service. Online games exploit the connectivity of the Internet, which appears to trigger rapid growth of the online game industry (OECD 2005). The online game industry is technology-intensive as well as the traditional video game industry and it depends on complementary technologies such as micro payments, broadband diffusions, and popularization of PCs (Lee et al. 2017). Traditional video games and online games are both experience goods, which means it is not easy to judge their value before use. Characteristics of experience goods make it difficult for managers and investors of game industries to allocate human and monetary resources.

This paper measures the impacts of the government enforcement to reveal the online game specification that can reduce information asymmetry by applying real option theory before the commercialization procedure. Online games are usually updated periodically, and the updates contain new features. So, we test information asymmetry for the beginning of commercialization and the updates that contain less information than the beginning period of the game. We adopt the event study methodology to discover reactions of stock markets during the online game development process.

Understanding information spillovers to the stock market during the product development cycle will provide a signal to investors and people who are interested in this product. By analyzing the information spillovers, the market may accordingly change the present value of undergoing products. So the related matters of information spillovers of online games (i.e. when they happen, what is included, which steps are important, or which steps are voluntary or forced by law) is critical to policy makers for the transparency of the online game industry.

2   Conceptual Background and Hypotheses

2.1   Online Game Characteristics

Network Effects of Games. Usually a massively multiplayer online games (MMOG) consists of two key components: a seamless vast virtual world and a large number of multiple users. The virtual world is evolved in real time through interactions of the users. Massive user connectivity, interactivity, and a continuing virtual world make it difficult to technically implement a MMOG game and require vast amounts of investments for development. On the contrary a conventional casual game creates disposable virtual spaces and a number of 2–32 clients participate in the game that is hosted in such spaces. At the end of a game session these virtual spaces are removed, and the results of the game are saved in the central databases.

Meagher and Teo (2005) modeled the existence of network externality in multi playable online games (MPOGs) using a two-part tariffs model. The model in this study is consistent with observed examples of online games pricing strategies.

Traditional video games are based on their dedicated platform, and their strategies contribute to the survival of indirect network externalities by increasing third parties to produce games for their platforms. But most online games do not have dedicated platforms. Online games generally make use of a personal computer and the Internet broadband. Choi and Kim (2004) showed that not only personal interactions and playing, but also anticipation of social interactions help players to reach flow. Steinkuehler and Williams (2006) said that "by providing spaces for social interactions and relationships. MMOs have the capacity to function as one form of a new 'third place' for informal sociability." Many people anticipate relationships when they choose to play an online game. A player will have more utility when s/he selects an online game in which more players participate. This feature may generate direct network effects: as more people participate in a game, a player will be bestowed with more utility.

The Korean Game Rating Board examines game contents, and rates it with one of the following 4 rates: "Everyone", "Above 12", "Above 15", and "Adults only (above 18)". "Everyone" graded games can be played by any players, including potential players of "Above 12", "Above 15", and "Adults only (above 18)" graded games. But "Adults only (above 18)" grade games are only playable by players who are older than eighteen. The difference of potential players between "Everyone" and "Adults only (above 18)" graded games reduces the pool of potential players from 100% to 67.8% (Korea Creative Contents Agency 2012). "Adults only (above 18)" online games contain generally prohibited activities in the reality such as violent, sexual, bleeding, or drug-use related actions; these contents may prevent potential players from playing the game, if they do not personally prefer some of these contents. Hence, the positive network externality in online game suggests that the direct network externality induces online games to gain more potential players which leads to a higher stock price reaction.

H1: If an online game has more potential players, then it promotes a higher stock price reaction of the firm which serves the game in the market.

Experience Goods. Many MMOGs offer trial opportunities for players in limited level or time, but basically MMOGs adopted subscription-based pricing strategies. Casual games use more aggressive strategies: they offer basic game functions for free and charge for optional game items (item-based pricing) such as beautiful hats, pets, or functional items: for example, strengthening their avatar for 5 min. If many games operate for free, subscription-based payments acts as an entry barrier for players. A game which does not charge for access is attractive. Traditional video games, including online games, are typical experience goods. Gaining information about quality of experience goods differs from getting information about the price of experience goods, and the latter is easy and inexpensive to obtain. It is also expected that the variance in the quality of the experience a player gets to be greater than the variance in the utility of price (Nelson 1970). It is easy to guess the quality of casual games because casual games are generally based on the real activities such as sports, racing, or dancing. On the other hand, an MMOG has its unique background, user interfaces, and its systems.

Usually casual games have much simpler structures and logics than MMOGs. The simplicity and aggressive pricing strategies of casual games makes it much easier for potential players to discover their values in fewer sampling trials. So we can assume the following hypothesis:

H2: Introduction of casual games will have a larger impact on stock prices than MMOGs.

Longer Life Expectancy of Online Games. Lineage and Lineage 2, popular online games developed by NCSoft, have been running over 15 and 10 years respectively. A casual game, the "Crazy Arcade" developed and serviced by Nexon, is also enjoying a long life of 12 years. Many online games enjoy a longer lifespan than video games. Online games have average 50.8-month lifetime, but video games have only up to a 24-month lifetime, less than a half of an online game lifetime (Korea Creative Contents Agency 2012). It is well known that traditional video games follow the box office revenue models of Hollywood "blockbusters": 80% of the total revenues are made in the initial month, after which revenues quickly decline on a weekly basis. The average shelf-life of a video game is about six weeks. On the other hand, online game revenues increase over time: routine and urgent updates make its life time longer (Choi et al. 2007).

The major reason why online games usually have longer lifecycles is that they receive routine updates. A routine update generally adds new contents to the existing game and fixes its bugs. Major updates are usually applied one or two times a year; they add whole new story portions, tweak existing game systems, and eventually enhance the gaming experiences with improved game engine features and user interfaces. Minor updates are generally done between one or two weeks; they may add holiday events, minor story additions, and bug fixes.

So reacting to players' demands and to solve unintended situations such as bugs to hinder players' activities or system abuse is not only crucial to the success of an online game but also to sustaining a long life time of the game (Meagher and Teo 2005). According to the aforementioned logic, we can expect that a firm having game maintenance capability produces higher market reactions in the online game industry than a firm without it.

H3: A firm which has game maintenance and development capability can expect higher market reactions than a firm without it.

Business models in the online game industry. We focus on the "dis-intermediated" firms which are vertical integrated firms. These firms appeared in the beginning era of the online game industry. These firms have developmental organizations and service operation departments. They develop their own games, distribute them in their game portal, do marketing campaigns, and serve their games by themselves. It is platform providers that are similar to vertically integrated firms in the video game industry such as Sony, Microsoft, and Nintendo. In the traditional video game market, platform providers differentiate themselves by incompatible hardware systems (Aoyama and Izushi 2003) and the exclusive killer titles such as "Super Mario" which was only playable on Nintendo platforms. Platform providers focus on gathering competent independent developers that do not own a platform. Gathering third-parties (competent independent developers) reinforces indirect network effects based on its platform (Zhu and Iansiti 2012). One more reason is "software licensing fees are the primary source of revenue for platform providers" of the video game industry. So platform providers prefer to gather more third-party developers. The online game firms, however, adopt vertical integration in order to operate their own games by themselves and to earn money directly through the service of these online games to reduce transaction costs.

Many online game projects are high risk projects with high returns. From this point of view, online games can be viewed the same way as high risk R&D projects. Online game firms may stop their projects if they predict that it will not yield the initially targeted profits. The publisher, developer, and vertical integrated model have differences in real options when the project outcome is uncertain.

A vertically integrated firm can enjoy various real options: they may either stop the project, simply delay it, or may acquire a firm which develops an online game or is able to develop new projects for their line-up. But for an independent publisher it is not easy to delay a project or develop a new one. Similarly, an independent developer has the options to stop, delay its projects or develop a new one, but the actions are limited by contracts with a publisher. They do not have the real options of acquiring new projects that are under development or developed by others. Independent publishers cannot take actions without help from the developer's side regarding problems such as bugs or unexpected events. Most independent online game publishers started without online game development teams, so they did not have sufficient experience to solve unexpected technical problems that occurred when online games were served to the public in the early stage. So it is predictable that a firm which adopts vertically integration receives higher stock returns from the market.

H4: Vertically integrated firms show higher stock returns than independent developers or independent publishers.

3 Data and Method

We collect data from Korean online game industry during 2002–2009. The history of the Korean online game industry is the longest in the world, and the Korean market is still a leading global market. By using data collected in the early stage of the industry life cycle, we can generalize the results to other countries who need to understand the policy implications before they introduce regulatory frameworks.

There were 12 firms listed on the Korean stock market in 2009. One firm, NCSoft is listed on KSE, the others on KOSDAQ. We selected firms which have an online game business as the major part in their portfolios. We gathered disclosures from the website of the Korean Financial Supervisory Service for all 12 firms to control confounding effects, especially financial issues. We retrieve the game rating information from the Korean Game Rating Board website. We dropped GameHI and JCEntertainment data. These two firms were listed in 2009, so it was not enough to calculate normal returns. So we used ten firms for the event study test. The sample size of this study is small, but Brown and Warner (1985) showed that the specification of the test statistics is not dramatically altered if sample size is less than 20 compared to 50 in their sensitivity analysis.

Press releases contain broad information such as: announcements of a new online game development; announcements of close beta tests and open beta tests; commercialization schedules, promotions of upkeep and new online games; and update notices of upkeep games. We chose Yonhap News Agency as a source of press releases because

Yonhap News provides the most comprehensive database of news, other printed information, and press releases. This database provides press releases from January 2004 to May 2009. We supplemented them from the firm's own website when necessary.

The Korean Game Rating Board is a regulatory agency granting rates for computer game publications. It is the Game Industry Promotional Act enacted in 2006 that prevents the publishing of a game without a rating. The Game Rating Board demands expressions and substances of sustaining coherence to retain a rating. If expressions or the substances of a game are changed without prior notice, the board has the authority to suspend any further commercial/non-commercial service.

We acquired game rating information from the website of the Game Rating Board. All the game rating information of our targets are available after 2000. For this study we only included data regarding online games. We excluded new games or sequels in the other gaming platforms such as mobile and video game platforms. As of 2008, there were a total of 4,426 cases requesting the game rating. 3,375 cases (76.25%) received an "Everyone" grade and 749 cases (16.92%) were granted an "Adults only" grade. The "Above 12" and "Above 15" grades only took up very small portions of the total cases, just 184 (4.15%) and 118 (2.67%) respectively. Due to their small portions we did our tests only with the "Everyone" and "Adults only (above 18)" cases.

After the data gathering, we deleted invalid events that lacked sufficient event window spans of at least three days (event day ± 1 day). Publishers generated press releases for their individual games on the daily basis. So many press releases about updates and promotions of the games have less than three days. Filtering procedure to remove overlapped events for the game rating is similar to the press release. However game rating is less frequent than the press release, deleted events percentages of the game rating is less than the percentages of the press release.

Many studies used event study methodology for extracting the reactions between events and stock price changes. Event study was first adopted in the finance sectors (Dodd and Warner 1983).

We adopted the traditional assumptions on the event study method: efficient market hypothesis, unanticipated events, and confounding effects (McWilliams and Siegel 1997). In this study, we adopted the traditional event study that was used in McWilliams and Siegel (1997) and Im et al. (2001). It is a standard residual analysis technique based on the market model. We set the event day as $t = 0$, which is shown in press releases or game ratings information. The trading day prior to event day is numbered as minus, $t = -1$, $t = -2$, and trading day after event day set as plus, $t = +1$, $t = +2$. We estimated daily market model parameters for each event using two hundred day returns from $t = -250$ to $t = -51$. Similar studies generally use two hundred days to estimate normal returns.

$$R_{it} = \alpha_i + \beta_i R_{m,t} + \varepsilon_{i,t} \tag{1}$$

Regression (1) is used to estimate the coefficients of the daily market model. Rit is the common stock return of firm i on day t calculated by (2), and Rmt is the market return on day t calculated by (3). Because the common stock return, Rit, and the market return, Rmt, are evaluated as the difference of each price respectively, we do not put the control variables in the regression (1). Two parameters, ai and bi, are ordinary least squares estimators, and εit is the market model error.

$$R_{it} = \frac{price_{i,t} - price_{i,t-1}}{price_{i,t-1}} \tag{2}$$

$$R_{mt} = \frac{price_{m,t} - price_{m,t-1}}{price_{m,t-1}} \tag{3}$$

In this study, we calculated abnormal returns from the difference between the expected return of market returns at time t and individual firm i's returns at time t that is calculated in (4). The standard errors are calculated by the formula defined by Im et al. (2001).

$$AR_{i,t} = R_{i,t} - (\alpha_i + \beta_i R_{m,t}) \tag{4}$$

$$var(AR_{i,\tau}) = \left(S_i^2 \left[1 + \frac{1}{T} \frac{(R_{m,\tau} - \overline{R_m})^2}{\sum\limits_{t=1}^{T} (R_{m,t} - \overline{R_m})^2} \right] \right) \tag{5}$$

We used the cumulative abnormal return (CAR) values for specified window sizes that contain event days. We used (6) to calculate the cumulative abnormal return (CAR) for various window sizes. τ and τ' can be different if the window size is not symmetric. Under the assumption that the returns on each day are independent, the standard error of the cumulative return is the sum of the standard errors (Subramani and Walden 2001).

$$CAR_{i,\tau} = \sum_{i=-\tau}^{\tau} AR_{i,i} \tag{6}$$

$$var(CAR_{i,\tau}) = \sum_{j=-\tau}^{\tau} var(AR_{i,j}) \tag{7}$$

As this study is the first trial event study about the online game industry, a field where this method has never been applied, we tried several window sizes: $t = -1\sim1$, $t = -3\sim3$, $t = -5\sim1$, $t = -5\sim5$, $t = -10\sim1$, and $t = -10\sim10$ to determine which one would be appropriate empirically. We tested asymmetric windows due to the issue of information leakage. If any information is leaked, asymmetric windows should show higher returns than other windows. Through testing six window sizes, we finally adopted three windows sizes in order to achieve bigger cumulative abnormal returns than other returns. The adopted sizes are: $t = -3\sim3$, $t = -5\sim1$ and $t = -5\sim5$. An asymmetric window was accepted to reveal information leakage. In the results, the values of cumulative abnormal returns (CAR) of the asymmetric window are superior compared to symmetric windows.

$$\overline{CAR_\tau} = \frac{1}{N} \sum_{i=1}^{N} CAR_{i,\tau} \tag{8}$$

$$\text{var}(\overline{CAR_\tau}) = \frac{1}{N^2} \sum_{i=1}^{N} \text{var}(CAR_{i,\tau}) \tag{9}$$

Finally, we employed a conventional t-test for the significance test with average standardized cumulative abnormal return (ASCAR) and its variance.

$$t = \frac{\overline{CAR_\tau}}{\sqrt{\text{var}(\overline{CAR_\tau})}} \sim t_{(\alpha, df\, =\, N\, -\, 1)} \tag{10}$$

We took stock market index and daily stock price information of our target firms from Fnguide.com. We utilized a rectified stock price of each firm provided by this web site. As we assumed two hundred days as the daily market model estimation time, two firms did not achieve these criteria and we could not analyze them. Neowiz Holdings announced in 2007 they would divide their online game business division into Neowiz Games. But Neowiz Holdings kept governing Neowiz Games even after being listed in KOSDAQ as a separate firm. So we only analyzed Neowiz Holdings data and excluded Neowiz Games from our analysis with the purpose of avoiding duplication and maintaining stock price consistency.

$$AR_{i,t} = (R_{i,t} - R_{free,t}) - (\alpha + \beta(R_{m,t} - R_{free,t})) \tag{11}$$

We use another estimation model to control macroeconomic influences: capital asset pricing model, the Eq. (11). We adopted the three year Korean government bond rate as the risk free rate. The results of the CAPM model is almost similar to the market model. It also supports the robustness of our results.

4 Results

Table 1 presents average cumulative abnormal return (ACAR) values of our estimated three different window sizes associated with online game development and publishing events. The numbers inside the parenthesis represent p-values respectively. We display the level of p-values as asterisks next to the parentheses: a value that is $p < 0.10$ represents cross (†), values that are $p < 0.05$ are represented with one asterisk (*), and values that fall under $p < 0.01$ are depicted as two asterisks (**).

Regarding our overall observations, we conclude that game rating events have significant meanings. In the case of game rating event, ACARs shows positive and significant values for unbalanced window $t = -5$ to $t = 1$. On the other hand, press releases are insignificant. An important premise of this research is that generally stock price reactions to game rating events will show significantly positive values rather than zero. The information from a game rating is regarded as a signal of the possibility that the product will be introduced into the market and also includes an outline of the game.

Many investors and managers inferred that each beta test and the final commercialization of a product would raise the firm value: this assumption does not fit with our results. Usually plenty of media reports already deliver related information before press releases to the market before beta tests are conducted or commercialized. We guess that

Table 1. Stock price reactions to online game events

Event classification	Window size (in days)	$-3 \sim +3$	$-5 \sim +1$	$-5 \sim +5$
Stock price reactions	Game rating	.0016 (.119)	.00178 (.091)†	.0014 (.105)
	Press release	.0001 (.396)	−.0004 (.371)	−.0010 (.177)
Reactions to game rating by age grades	Everyone	.0035 (.039)*	.0039 (.025)*	.0036 (.013)*
	Adults only	−.0003 (.389)	−.0009 (.334)	−.0010 (.307)
Reactions to game rating by category	MMOGs	.0002 (.394)	.0011 (.297)	.0005 (.372)
	Casual game	.0026 (.065)†	.0024 (.087)†	.0029 (.024)*
Reactions to game rating by business structure	Vertical integration	.0015 (.239)	.0014 (.242)	.0019 (.128)
	Independent developer	.0029 (.130)	.0043 (.041)*	.0033 (.056)†
	Independent publisher	.0002 (.392)	−.0010 (.348)	−.0035 (.070)†
Reactions to press release by business structure	Vertical integration	.0017 (.116)	.0002 (.391)	.0001 (.394)
	Independent developer	−.0024 (.175)	−.0043 (.389)	−.0015 (.229)
	Independent publisher	−.0021 (.178)	−.0037 (.194)	−.0038 (.122)

*: $p < .05$, **: $p < .01$, †: $p < 0.10$. The value in the parentheses is p-value. Less than .001 reported as $< .001$.

lots of media reports leak related information about new games and as an effect reduces the abnormal return on the actual event days. These events can be interpreted as earning shocks if the real earning of a firm in the annual report is less the same as to the expectation of the earning. All information is already leaked and the information is realized as a price of the stock.

Game rating events were tested according to the rating grade the game has received. The results are also summarized in Table 1. We found that all ACARs of "Everyone" rates are positive and show significant values for all event window sizes. We guess that this result mainly stems from the existence of direct network externality. The smaller potential customer size of the "Adults only" grade is one of the main reasons to show negative ACARs, which is not significant. Another reason is the diversity of preferences of adult users. Many people develop their own tastes while growing up. So many "Everyone" grade online games have similar appearance as they have the same large pool of potential users; whereas "Adults only" rated online games mostly contain different contents. This leads to the result that the "Everyone" rated games have bigger potentials than "Adult only" rated games. This result can be interpreted as a sign that as direct network externality exists in online games, which supports our Hypothesis 1.

To test Hypothesis 2 by stock price reactions to game ratings that are classified according to categories, we received the following expected result: stock price reactions to game ratings of casual games are positive and show significant values. So we can accept hypothesis 2. As opposed to the results of casual games, stock price reactions to game ratings of MMOGs do not show any significance. Due to the simple game structure and contents, relatively small sizes that make them easy to download and install, casual games can usually gather more attention in a given short time compared to MMOGs. It is reasonable to assume that many investors are also able to make proper decisions within a shorter time about casual games compared to cases of MMOGs.

If the Korean market just preferred the casual games, then the new portfolio which contains casual games for each grade, "Everyone" and "Adult only", will show positive and significant stock returns respectively. But the results do not match this opinion. Table 2 shows the results for casual games. As we expected with Hypothesis 1, casual games with the "Everyone" grade which have more potential players show positive and significant stock returns. Casual games which rated "Adult only" show no significant relationship with stock returns. We also did the same tests for MMOGs, but all rated MMOGs show no significant relationship with stock returns.

Table 2. ACAR for casual games

Event windows	ACAR casual games	
	Everyone	Adult only
−3− + 3	.00385(.040)*	.00017(.395)
−5− + 1	.00455(.017)*	.00051(.382)
−5− + 5	.00411(.017)*	.00037(.385)

We can see that independent developers show positive and significant impacts on stock reactions to game ratings by business structure in Table 1. But vertically integrated firms do not show significant stock returns. So we partially accept Hypothesis 3. Because of the important technological aspects of the industry, the development capability is considered as an important factor in the online game industry. The reason that independent developers are seeing higher stock price reaction than other models lies in the timing of capitalization: independent developers can capitalize some part of the expected total earnings by licensing the product to the publisher, but firms which adopted the vertical integration model have to pay additional costs for beta tests, marketing campaigns, and commercial distribution. Generally vertically integrated firms are able to capitalize larger amounts of financial resources for a game than other models, but the realization of such a capitalization takes more time than firms which adopted the independent developer model.

We proposed the impacts of business models in the online game industry with Hypothesis 4. Against our expectations, vertically integrated firms did not show higher stock returns than other business models.

5 Conclusions

This paper found that not only online game characteristics but also the online game industry structure that is favorable to market reactions. The findings of this paper have strategic implications to policy makers and online game makers.

We derived the following results. First, it is likely for online games to have direct network externalities generated by interactions within potential players. Its managerial implication is that the firms pay more attentions to boost network externalities through interactions in the game to ensure their success in the online game industry. Sustaining development ability (or technological competence) is an important factor in the online game industry. Online games are complex experience goods: they are technology-intensive, but the contents are also important (Choi et al. 2007). Continuous technological innovation and maintenance with technological competence can make differences to competitors. Hence, the independent publishers may be seriously disadvantaged in this industry than in the traditional video game industry. The downtime of World of Warcraft in China was due to a change-over in the Chinese game operation license regulation. This was an inevitable incident to Activision-Blizzard. It is an example that an independent publisher can suffer in the market.

Casual games, which are generally simpler than MMOGs, generate stronger market reactions in the short term due to ease of quality evaluation, possibly the shorter payback cycle of investments and smaller capital requirements for development, all of which lead to lower risks. But it does not mean that casual games show superior performance in the long run. High stock returns in the short term do not guarantee high performance in the long term. Stronger market reactions of the casual games could be based on the market preference, but it is not easy to identify market preference publicly. We pooled casual games and MMOGs in this study. However, as mentioned before, MMOGs have much longer service cycles and more various pricing strategies after our data period. Therefore, MMOGs may require studies over a much longer time.

We studied relationships between events and stock price reactions only. Linking market responses to actual game success may be an interesting topic to be explored further. As we tested in this game, many online games are launched in the market every year, while many online games are withdrawn from the market. That may test the efficiency of financial markets in assessing online games' success in the market.

While our study is limited to online games, expansion to other entertainment genres may shed more light on similarities and dissimilarities of the online game industry against traditional entertainment markets.

References

Delmas, M., Montes-Sacho, M.J., Shimshack, J.P.: Information disclosure policies: evidence from the electricity industry. Econ. Inq. **48**(2), 483–498 (2010)

Verrecchia, R.E.: Policy implications from the theory-based literature on disclosure. The Economics and Politics of Accounting, pp. 149–163 (2004)

Skouloudis, A., Malesios, C., Dimitrakopoulos, P.: Corporate biodiversity accounting and reporting in mega-diverse countries: an examination of indicators disclosed in sustainability reports. Ecol. Ind. **98**, 888–901 (2019)

OECD. 2005. The online computer and video game industry (OECD, 1ed.), pp. 1–68 (2005)

Lee, D., Lee, S., Kim, J.H.: Analysis on the evolution and innovation of online game industry using meta-frontier analysis. Asian J. Technol. Innov. **25**, 158–167 (2017)

Meagher, K., Teo, E.G.S.: Two-part tariffs in the online gaming industry: the role of creative destruction and network externalities. Inf. Econ. Policy **17**(4), 457–470 (2005)

Choi, D., Kim, J.: Why people continue to play online games: in search of critical design factors to increase customer loyalty to online contents. Cyber Psychol. Behav. **7**(1), 11–24 (2004)

Steinkuehler, C.A., Williams, D.: Where everybody knows your (screen) name: online games as "third places". J. Comput.-Mediat. Commun. **11**(4), 885–909 (2006)

Korea Creative Contents Agency. White Paper on Korean Games, pp. 1–980 (2012)

Nelson, P.: Information and consumer behavior. J. Polit. Econ. **78**(2), 311–329 (1970)

Choi, J.-S., Lee, S., Ha, T. J., Hong, Y. J., Lee, Y. H., Jung, J.Y.: Innovation characteristics and R&D strategies in creative service industries: online games in Korea, pp. 1–543 (2007)

Aoyama, Y., Izushi, H.: Hardware gimmick or cultural innovation? Technological, cultural, and social foundations of the Japanese video game industry. Res. Policy **32**(3), 423–444 (2003)

Zhu, F., Iansiti, M.: Entry into platform-based markets. Strateg. Manag. J. **33**(1), 88–106 (2012)

Dodd, P., Warner, J.B.: On corporate governance: a study of proxy contests. J. Financ. Econ. **11**(1–4), 401–438 (1983)

McWilliams, A., Siegel, D.: Event studies in management research: theoretical and empirical issues. Acad. Manag. J. **40**(3), 626–657 (1997)

Im, K.S., Dow, K.E., Grover, V.: Research report: a reexamination of IT investment and the market value of the firm–an event study methodology. Inf. Syst. Res. **12**(1), 103–117 (2001)

Subramani, M., Walden, E.: The impact of E-commerce announcements on the market value of firms. Inf. Syst. Res. **12**(2), 135–154 (2001)

Brown, S.J., Warner, J.B.: Using daily stock returns: The case of event studies. J. Financ. Econ. **14**(1), 3–31 (1985)

User Perspectives

Analysing Legal Information Requirements for Public Policy Making

Charalampos Alexopoulos[1]([⊠]), Shefali Virkar[2] [iD], Michalis Avgerinos Loutsaris[1], Anna-Sophie Novak[2], and Euripidis Loukis[1]

[1] University of the Aegean, Samos, Greece
{alexop,mloutsaris,eloukis}@aegean.gr
[2] Danube University Krems, Krems an der Donau, Austria
{shefali.virkar,anna-sophie.novak}@donau-uni.ac.at

Abstract. Most of the research that has been conducted in the area of legal informatics concerns its 'supply side', dealing with the development of effective systems for legal information provision. However, limited research has been conducted on the 'demand side' of legal information provision, though it is absolutely necessary to gain a good understanding of it, in order to design effective and useful systems for the provision of legal information; furthermore, this limited research is dealing with the legal information needs of the lawyers, and neglects the ones of other important groups. This paper contributes to filling this research gap. It analyses legal information requirements of a highly important for the society group: the designers of public policies. Initially we investigate current legal information sources and systems used by public policy makers, as well as their relevant search practices. Then we investigate their business needs for additional capabilities/functionalities for a better support of their policymaking activities using advanced legal analytics tools and services. Finally, we discuss the information, processing and technical requirements for the development of a legal information system providing the above advanced functionalities and services. For the above purposes, we have collected data through semi-structured interviews form 13 Greek and 7 Austrian public administrators dealing with the design of public policies, which lead to interesting and useful insights, as well as a novel set of additional advanced capabilities and functionalities that can give rise to a new generation of legal informatics.

Keywords: Legal information · Legal informatics · Public policy · Decision support systems · Service provision

1 Introduction

Recent trends in digitalization, open data, and social media have resulted in an exponential increase in the amount of data available for use by public policy makers in order to make sense of the socio-economic and political phenomena, and design relevant public policies [1]. Repositories of large quantities of novel types of information – including

S. Hofmann et al. (Eds.): ePart 2020, LNCS 12220, pp. 95–108, 2020.
https://doi.org/10.1007/978-3-030-58141-1_8

expert knowledge, sensor data, text, social media posts - have become available to policy makers. An important part of this information, which is highly useful and important for policy makers, is legal information, concerning existing or previous relevant legislation, both of their country as well as other countries, and also European legislation. Advanced intelligent systems, together with sophisticated techniques of data harvesting, annotation, analysis and visualisation have enhanced our ability to understand and make sense of extensive and complex relevant information to policy makers.

Complex decision-making based on the profound analysis of societal problems and possible solutions using these large quantities of available data is a prominent aspect and target of evidence-based policymaking. However, policy makers are currently confronted with the challenge of accessing vast, hitherto untapped, sources of information in an efficient manner that provides all relevant information, separates 'noise' from 'signal', and assists and supports them substantially for designing effective public policies. Furthermore, policy makers are also not equipped with the skills and technical know-how necessary to integrate and process all relevant information, including the most current data, from various sources, and elicit meaning from it, in order to make informed policy decisions. The solution to the above problems is the development of advanced decision support systems that exploit available big data in order to facilitate the cognitive activity involved in the structuring of public policy decision situations, the design of policy options, the enumeration of alternative courses of action, and the evaluation of these alternatives leading to a policy decision. Until recently, these tools have been time-consuming to deploy, and also not user-friendly for decision makers, and frequently resulting in models that do not reflect 'real-life' policy realities [2].

This paper presents research conducted towards addressing the above challenges, for one of the most important and at the same time difficult to manage kinds of information needed for supporting policy making, the legal information, as part of the European 'ManyLaws' project [3]. The objective of this project is to develop advanced decision support tools and services for policy actors built on a robust foundation of legal information search retrieval. It aims to offer users a suite of targeted services to support policy making through the provision of advanced legal information, built upon semantic analysis techniques, text mining tools, and in general advanced processing technologies. For this purpose, it is necessary to examine critically how decision-making activities within the policymaking process might be supported through improved legal information search and retrieval capabilities.

However, these requirements have not been sufficiently researched. As explained in more detail in Sect. 2.2 most of the research that has been conducted in the area of legal informatics concerns its 'supply side', dealing with the development of effective systems for legal information provision, with advanced search and processing capabilities, based on appropriate metadata as well as organization and annotation of large quantities of textual legal information. On the contrary, limited research has been conducted on the 'demand side' of legal information provision, though it is absolutely necessary to gain a good understanding of it, in order to design effective and useful systems for the provision of legal information. Furthermore, as concluded in Sect. 2.2, this limited research is dealing with the legal information needs of the lawyers and neglects the ones of other important groups. Therefore, this paper contributes to filling this important research gap.

It analyses legal information requirements of a highly important for the society group: the designers of public policies. In particular, we investigate the following research questions:

- RQ1. What are the current legal information sources and systems used by public policy makers, as well as their relevant search practices?
- RQ2. What are the business needs of policy makers needs for additional capabilities/functionalities for having a better support of their policymaking activities using advanced legal analytics tools and services?
- RQ3. What are the information, processing and technical requirements for the development of an information system providing the above advanced functionalities and services?

Our study has been based on the collection of data through interviews with 13 Greek and 7 Austrian public administrators dealing with the design of public policies.

This paper is structured in six sections. The following Sect. 2 critically discusses decision making and decision support tools within the context of public policy creation, as well as legal information provision and analytics. Next, Sect. 3 outlines the methodological approach we adopted in order to collect primary data. Section 4 then presents the results of the abovementioned in-depth expert interviews with policymakers from Greece and Austria. Emerging themes and issues are analysed in Sect. 5, and finally conclusions and recommendations for future research are outlined in Sect. 6.

2 Background

2.1 Decision Support Systems and the Public Policy Cycle

Decision support systems (DSS) constitute a class of advanced computer systems comprising a collection of software applications and tools developed in order to facilitate managerial decision making and improve the quality of the decisions being taken - particularly under conditions of uncertainty, initially in the private sector, but later in the public sector as well [4]. These systems facilitate the co-ordination of data delivery and the development of data consistency, aid in data trend analysis as well as use for making forecasts, fulfilling users' data requirements, and supporting the quantification of uncertainty, as well as recommending courses of action [5]. [6] identifies seven different types of DSS applications, based on contemporary professional practice and actor-base: Personal Decision Support Systems, Group Support Systems, Negotiation Support Systems, Intelligent Decision Support Systems, Knowledge Management-based DSS, Data Warehousing, and Enterprise Reporting and Analysis Systems. Furthermore, they argue that among them the personal decision support systems, data warehousing, and enterprise reporting and analysis systems are the most widely available and used systems in day-to-day contexts. [5] identify a number of Artificial Intelligence paradigms that can be used in order to mimic complex human problem-solving behaviour that is otherwise difficult to describe mathematically using conventional programming methods (using symbolic logic, Artificial Neural Networks (ANNs), fuzzy systems, evolutionary computing, Intelligent Agents, and probabilistic reasoning models, etc.).

In order to fully understand the implications of developing a decision support system to facilitate the formulation of effective public policy, which is the main target of our research, it is important to understand the nature of the policy-making process, and the main practical challenges that the creation of public policy presents. According to [7], the public policy process includes one or more cycles, each of them including the following stages: agenda setting, policy formulation, decision-making, policy implementation, policy evaluation and finally policy improvement/maintenance or termination. Implicit in this conceptualisation is the progression of the different stages in a distinct chronological order: to begin with, problems are defined and placed on the agenda; next policies are developed, adopted and implemented; and finally, select policies are evaluated and either terminated or pursued further [8]. The cyclical framing of the policymaking process underlines the manner in which a feedback loop is created between its various inputs and outputs, punctuated by decision points, resulting in a policy outcome [9]. The legislation-oriented DSS under development in this research project aims to support all the above stages of policy of policy making with respect to legal information provision, based on advanced techniques concerning how the legal information is handled, processes, semantically annotated, presented and accessed.

2.2 Legal Information Provision and Analytics

Legal Informatics refer to the application of Information and Communication Technologies (ICT) within the context of legal environment [10], and is defined by [11] as the "...theory and practice of computable law, i.e. the cooperation between humans and machines in legal problem-solving". This area focuses on the opportunities and challenges that the exploitation of ICT in the legal system faces, and thus involves all related organizations and legal information users in the legal domain. One of these challenges lies in the supply of legal services, which are currently under-consumed by individuals and companies [12]. Therefore, the latest advancements in the legal informatics are targeted towards making services more open and promoting access to legal resources.

Furthermore, accurate and timely legal information is an essential component of effective decision-making by several different societal actors. However, the ability of citizens, businesses, public servants as well as politicians and their advisers to easily access, fully comprehend and apply complex legal information to their everyday contexts often hinges on an advanced understanding of governmental procedures, legal language, and the law itself. Unfortunately, usually this does not happen, and most people struggle and have difficulties to locate the legal artefacts they need. On a practical level, two immediate problems can be identified. The first pertains to the quantity of legal information currently available online, as a direct consequence of the increasing complexity of the European legal system, coupled with advances in digital technologies, cloud storage capabilities and the Open Data movement. The second problem concerns users' ability to comprehend legal information, as well as the singular nature of legal jargon, wherein most individuals do not possess the specialist legal education and practical knowledge required to grasp complex legal terminology or follow developments in legislative processes. Both these phenomena have resulted in the burgeoning popularity of legal analytics, or the application of big data analysis methods within the field of the law [13], which has, within a very short span of time, moved from the margins of the legal profession into the mainstream.

Recently, an important trend in the area of legal informatics is the increasing exploitation of artificial intelligence technologies, as new legal applications based on text and natural language processing and machine learning have recently emerged, which seem to influence significantly and gradually transform the practice of the law [14]. These tools and services, support conceptual legal information retrieval and predictive legal analysis by connecting computational models of legal reasoning directly with legal text. The legal field, however, remains one of the most difficult domains for the application of automated text retrieval, as legal text retrieval is based primarily upon concepts, and not on the explicit wording in the document texts [15]. [16] argue that this is because legal concepts are not discrete, but instead are situated along "...a dynamic continuum between common sense terms, specific technical use, and professional knowledge, in an evolving institutional reality." Moreover, legal text retrieval has traditionally relied upon external knowledge sources such as thesauri and classification schemes, and the manual indexing of documents [17].

However, the research that has been conducted in the area of legal informatics concerns mainly its 'supply side', dealing with the development of effective systems for legal information provision, with advanced search and processing capabilities, based on appropriate metadata as well as organization and annotation of large quantities of textual legal information. On the contrary, limited research has been conducted on the 'demand side' of legal information provision, though it is absolutely necessary to gain a good understanding of it, in order to design effective and useful systems for the provision of legal information; furthermore, this limited research is dealing with the legal information needs of the lawyers, and to a much lower extent of the citizens (general public), however it neglects the ones of the policy makers, though they rely heavily on a wide range of legal information, and they are quite important for the society. Some early papers have focused on the demand for paper-based legal information sources. [18] investigates the legal information needs of the general public (citizens who are not lawyers), as well as the sources (paper-based ones) they use in order to fulfil these needs, and the role of the general and law libraries, and also of legal aid centres, on this. In [19] are investigated the legal information needs of lawyers, the main purposes they are searching legal information for, the types of information required, and also sources and ways (paper-based ones) for meeting these needs; they conclude that only large law firms have extensive legal libraries and therefore sufficient access to legal information, while this does not hold for smaller law firms: for them the only practical solution, due to the inherently large volume of legal information required is co-operation among such firms, or use of courts' legal libraries. Furthermore, there is some subsequent research focusing on the demand for electronic legal information sources. [20] and [21] examine existing online sources of legal information from users' perspectives, however focusing mainly on their usability, and secondarily on the types of legal content they offer, aiming to identify problems that reduce accessibility and effective use by the users. In [22] are investigated the legal information needs of law faculty for their teaching and research work, as well as the paper-based and online sources used by them, their relevant perceptions and also their computing skills. Recently [23] examines the perceptions of academic and practicing lawyers about existing online legal information resources, as well as the degree of satisfaction with them, the barriers to their effective use, and also relevant requirements for the design of better legal information systems. Therefore, since the existing previous literature concerning the 'demand side' (users) of legal informatics is limited, and focusing mainly on lawyers, further research is required for understanding the usage and search behaviour of current users, as well as the needs of existing and potential users, investigating different user groups; furthermore, it is necessary to conduct 'innovation-oriented' research in order to identify additional novel advanced capabilities/functionalities that can provide higher levels of relevant decision support and lead to a new generation of legal informatics. Our paper makes a contribution in this direction.

3 Methodological Approach

Fundamental to the successful construction of an effective decision support system is the elicitation of user requirements, and the subsequent accurate definition of hardware and software specifications [24, 25]. [26] describes a framework that enables the integration of agile design methods with user-focused design approaches, showing that agile user-centric design focuses on an iterative and rigorous collaborative development process [27]. Important techniques for this phase of requirements engineering include the questionnaire, interviews, use cases/scenarios, observation and social analysis, focus groups, and brainstorming [28, 29].

One of the most commonly applied techniques for requirements elicitation, the expert in-depth interview is defined by [30] as "...a one-to-one method of data collection that involves an interviewer and interviewee discussing specific topics in depth." Typically, in-depth interviews are used in research to seek information on individual personal experiences pertaining to a specific issue or topic [31]. In the context of user requirements elicitation, in-depth interviews may be thought of as 'conversations with a purpose' during which stakeholders and/or domain experts are questioned to elicit information about their current attitudes, patterns of behaviour, modes of practice, and needs or requirements in relation to the new system or application. In-depth interviews are considered as an efficient way to collect large amounts of uniform data quickly [28, 32]. Following [28], this technique was selected as a data collection instrument that enabled researchers to collect rich qualitative data from interview subjects that reflected their experiences with legal information search and retrieval, as well as their expectations, ideas, and opinions.

Within the context of this study, the authors conducted a series of *in-depth, semi-structured* interviews in Greece and Austria in early 2019. The purpose of the interviews was to investigate patterns of legal information access and use amongst public administrators in the two pilot countries, as well as to gain deeper insight into current policymaking and legislative methods and practices identifying specific user needs and business requirements. In total 20 semi-structured interviews were conducted. Thirteen of them (four male and nine female subjects) were individuals representing different functions and levels of Greek public administration between 28 March and 30 April 2019. Seven of them (three male and four female participants) were members of Austrian public administration and/or from private legal practice representing different functions between 15

Table 1. Expert interview guide

Section/Main Topic	Purpose
Introduction	Provision of global context - introduction to interviewee by local co-ordinator, establishment of background to proposed project, information about the purpose of the interview
A. Demographic questions	Basic questions to establish demographic context of interviewee, including familiarity with information technology
B. Policy creation - best practices, methods, and systems	Questions about current policy making and/or legislative processes within national context, step-by-step procedure from interviewee perspective including current role, nature of collaboration between different actors, current information technology systems used
C. Policy creation – requirement for legal information, search strategies employed	Questions about interviewee requirement for and use of legal information
D. Policy creation - sources of data	Further questions on legal information sources used currently used by interviewee, especially concerning preferred sources of legal data
E. Business needs identification	Questions to identify business needs for potential users, including about features missing from current sources of legal information and reasons for use/non-use of databases or platforms
Summary	Closing statement(s) by interviewer summarising key points arising during interview, time given for participants to clarify or add to previous input

March and 15 April 2019. Ages ranged between 22 years and 64 years old, with further details withheld from being reported to preserve anonymity. Interviews were facilitated remotely, via a digital communications platform, as well as in person, and the working language was English. All interview transcripts have subsequently been codified and analysed.

The interview schedule was derived based on the one used to collect data for the five initial user stories, and comprised of the following top-level topics: *demographic questions*; *policy creation - best practices, methods and systems*; *policy creation – requirement for legal information, search strategies employed*; *policy creation - sources of data;* and the *identification of business needs*. The results of the in-depth expert interviews with policymakers affiliated to the Hellenic and Austrian parliaments are reported in this research paper and further elucidated upon in the interview guide (see Table 1, *above*).

4 Results

The study reported in this research paper sought to identify and determine the exact nature of the legal information requirements of public policymakers with a view to designing an advanced legal information system that fulfilled these needs. Through a detailed analysis of interview data, researchers sought to assess the current legal information data sources and systems available to their sample population, together with the practices, strategies and tools used to obtain legal information. From this enquiry, it was expected that the business needs of policy makers and legal administrators to support their day-to-day activities could be extracted, and that a better understanding of the underlying technical requirements gained. A summary of the salient points raised during these interviews may be found in the Table 2 below.

Table 2. Summary of expert interview results

Topics	Greece	Austria
Best practices, methods and systems	• Variance in the Degree of Collaboration between Policymakers and Legal Experts. Great degree of disperse among organisational units • Basic Informational Input for Policymaking is both General and Specialised • Uniform Criteria for Determining the Relevance or Suitability of Information: trusted sources and easiness of understanding • Experience and Expertise is Key When Assessing, Comparing or Evaluating Legal Information	• List of Most Popular Platforms and Sources of Legal Information Online • Extent of Collaboration between Legal Experts and Policymakers in Austria is Uncertain • General Emphasis on Accurate, Timely and Robust Legal Information • General Characteristics of 'Useful' Legal Information Identified
Requirement for legal information, search strategies employed	• Types Searched-For Legal Information • Search Strategies Adopted to Obtain Relevant Results • Further Capability Desired While Searching for Legal Information • Correlation of legal artefacts • Comparative analysis of laws • Transposition of EU directives in the national legal system	• Wide Range in the Types of Searched-For Legal Information • Emphasis on Digital Legal Information Sources • Few Desired Abilities and Wished-for System Functionalities • Timeline analysis
Sources of data	• Current Sources of Legal Information and Reasons for Preference • Organisational Endorsement of Legal Data Sources • Mainly Legal Database applies fees, but users prefer to use a legal database based on open data sources	• Popular Online Sources of Legal Information in Austria • Reasons for Preference of Currently Used Sources • No Particular Organisational Endorsement of Legal Information Sources • General Absence of Subscription Fees • Importance of Open Legal Data Sources

(*continued*)

Table 2. (*continued*)

Topics	Greece	Austria
Business needs identification	• No Collaborative Software Available • Missing Features and Functionalities from Current Online Sources of Legal Information • Added-value Features Looked-for in Current Sources of Legal Information • Willingness to pay a Subscription Fee for a Comprehensive, All-Inclusive Legal Information Resource • Noteworthy Thoughts or Issues Arising	• Desired Features Missing from Current Legal Data Sources • General Ambivalence Towards Subscription Fees • Professional Challenges May Be Overcome Through Access to Better Legal Data • Facilitating Policymaking Through Improved Access to Legal Information • Monitor progress • Visualisation of accumulative results

4.1 Best Practices, Methods and Systems

In both Greece and Austria, interview participants reported differences in the manner in which policymakers collaborated with legal experts, and also a significant degree of uncertainty as to the extent of these interactions. Both sets of participants emphasised the importance of information – in particular, legal information – as a vital input in policymaking. However, they also highlighted the importance of expert knowledge and judgement in selecting information as an input in the policymaking process. Even in the case of Austria where a very sophisticated system exists, it is managed by hand-written information (data entry by the administrators). The legal systems in both cases do not fully support the administrative processes of handling parliamentary data.

4.2 Requirement for Legal Information, Search Strategies Employed

Interview participants from both countries mentioned their requirement for unfettered access to a wide range of legal information sources, with particular emphasis on digital resources. They discussed the search strategies currently used to locate and retrieve information from these databases and expressed the desire to possess advanced search and retrieval capabilities, including complex string searches and translation features, in order to fully optimise their use. The currently offered functionality is restricted to services of searching by keywords which are not semantically annotated and/or extracted with a way that could illustrate correlations or even show the history of a law and its changes in time. The absence of semantically annotated does not allow to provide useful advanced services, such as the estimation of the degree of transposition of an EU Directive into the national legal system.

4.3 Sources of Legal Data

When questioned about the sources of legal data currently used, and the reasons for their preference, interview respondents from both Greece and Austria were able to name popular sources of this sort of information, and justify their use within individual professional contexts. Participants from Greece differed from their counterparts in Austria in saying that one reason for their use of particular data sources was organisational endorsement. All participants emphasised the importance of open legal data sources.

4.4 Business Needs Identification

Interview participants were asked to identify those features, tools and services either missing from current legal information retrieval resources, or whose addition or removal would facilitate their professional activities. Both sets of participants noted an absence of collaborative software available to them. They also identified an absence of customisable content – personalised dashboard, individual history, saved or book-marked content – as key functionalities missing from current online legal resources. Participants from Austria believed that they would be able to overcome professional challenges through better access to legal information, and that the quality of policymaking would be thereby enhanced. They differed from their counterparts in Greece through expressing a general ambivalence to subscription fees, even if those were paid for by the organisation.

Even more, the interviewees reported on general capabilities they would like to have from such a DSS: parallel search in multiple EU member-state legal frameworks using simple keywords; the capability to assess the degree of transposition of an EU directive in national legislation; an indication of the national legislation relevant to each directive and the capacity to monitor the status of transpositions; tools to analyse references made to the European legislation within national laws; the ability to make comparative analyses of equivalent or relevant laws from different EU member states and between connected laws from the same member state; the functionality to monitor the progress and/or current status of a specific piece of national or European legislation, including preparatory acts and agreements, over time; a visual timeline analysis tool for all legal elements; the provision of geo-visualisations, text-related visualisations, and other common visual decision aids; visualisations of correlations, dependencies and conflicts between different laws; and other dedicated decision support services, such as impact assessment, for expert users. It is envisioned that these services, when used alone or in combination through the proposed project portal, would enable policymakers to construct accurate models of the legal environment circumscribing the problem under consideration, identify the various possible outcomes based on an in-depth understanding of relevant legal matters, and design policy outcomes that conform with the current legal framework.

5 Discussion

In order to create an effective legal information retrieval system which functions like a DSS that assists the policy making process, it is important to apply the design principles of systems integration. As a first step, the key factors involved in the policy process and central to the construction of appropriate tools and services were identified through a combination of desk-based research and in-depth expert interviews, which are:

1. The principle model of the policy decision making process, based on a critical evaluation of the policy cycle framework.
2. The methods adopted for the implementation of its components in each pilot country, from the perspective of the policy actors interviewed.
3. The central decision makers and other primary stakeholders, and the relationships among them.

Furthermore, based on the results presented in Sect. 4 of the research paper, the primary requirements for the proposed decision support system were extracted, and they have been categorised in three groups: Information Requirements, Processing Requirements and Technical Requirements. In the following paragraphs we are discussing a possible solution towards covering the business needs of the participants.

Information Requirements: The complexity of the policy making process, captured through the lens of different policy roles and job functions, warrants the regular making of decisions based on accurate and complete legal information. In practice, it was seen that policymakers use both legislative information (information on the current national legal framework, the exact status of specific pieces of legislation, or comparative analyses of two or more pieces of legislation), policy information (general background information, policy reports, data and expert analysis), and political information (public opinion through social media and dedicated e-consultation and e-participation platforms, or of support for a policy among legislators) to support or oppose policy alternatives, or to make evidence-based judgements. The actual routes of information acquisition may include individual policymaker research, policy staff collaborative activity, committee hearings, oversight activities, or interdepartmental transactions.

Processing Requirements: In order to cover the information requirements, the proposed solution will structure the legal documents based on legal ontologies such as ELI and AKN. These ontologies are focused on representing information of two different kinds of data: (a) the description of the basic information of a law when it is published, and (b) information for better support the parliamentary procedure. For this purpose, the back-end may utilise various text-mining techniques, such as information extraction by using Regular Expressions, Tokenization, Word clustering, Word stemming, Results filtering, Data cleansing, Word Vector (Term Occurrences), just to name the most important ones [33]. All these techniques will extract all the necessary information that will be used for annotating the data and building the necessary files. Particularly, Regular expressions will separate the body of the legal document in components (Sections, Parts, Chapters, Articles, Paragraphs) and they extract all the correlations that included in each component. The general background information will be represented by keywords that will be extracted by using Tokenization of the Legal Document Body, Filtering the Stopwords, Stemming or Clustering the words (depends on the language of the legal document) and by creating a word vector of the terms that will be presented in a legal document. The first words, usually, are the most important words of a specific legal document and gives in the policy maker and legislator the opportunity to understand easily the content of this legal document [33]. In addition, the above serialization of the techniques will be used for generating the n-grams of the legal document towards the support of finding the similar legal documents. Finally, social media and governments portals that are used for collaborating of every new legal document among governments and citizens will be used in order to retrieve all related comments. These comments will be processed and semantically analysed to help legislators and policy makers to better design citizen-centric policies and propose policy alternatives.

Technical Requirements: The above processing requirements need the usage of a High-Performance Computing (HPC) [34], since the need is to produce n-grams at the degree of 10 (10-grams) as well as to analyse and semantically annotate the legal basis of two countries and the EU along with their associate parliamentary information. Paralleliza-tion of resources should be also applied by using computational clusters. This kind of clusters provide the ability to analyse huge amounts of unstructured data in a distributed computing environment. As a result, we will receive the legal documents in a structured and annotated way. Finally, a dedicated translation component, like the e-Translation DSI will translate all these structured data in different languages allowing the comparison of legal texts between different languages.

6 Conclusions

The policy making environment in today's digital world is characterised by high com-plexity, which necessitates access to and processing of large amounts of many different kinds of information, in order to gain a deep understanding of the big problems and chal-lenges of modern societies, and design effective policies for addressing them. One of the most important kinds of required information for modern policy making is definitely the legal information. The comprehension and extraction of meaning from numerous specialised domain-specific legal texts and laws is quite difficult for policy makers who are not legal experts. So, it is quite important to develop advanced legal information provision systems, which can offer substantial assistance and support in the above pol-icy making legislation-related tasks. However, this presupposes a deep understanding of legal information requirements of public policy making.

In this direction in the previous sections of this paper initially we investigated current legal information sources and systems used by public policy makers, as well as their relevant search practices. Then we examined their business needs for additional more advanced capabilities/functionalities that provide a better support of their policymaking activities using advanced legal analytics tools and services. Based on the findings we defined the information, processing and technical requirements for the development of a legal information system providing the above advanced functionalities and services. Our analysis has led to interesting and useful insights, as well as a novel set of additional advanced information provision capabilities and functionalities that can give rise to important innovations in the area of legal informatics, and finally to the emergence of a new generation of it. They include parallel search in multiple EU member-state legal frameworks using simple keywords, in order to identify and compare national legislations concerning a policy-related topic of interest, and capabilities for finding interconnections as well as conflicts among laws, as well as assessing the degree of transposition of an EU directive into national legislation, and visualizing results.

A limitation of our study is that it is based on interviews with a small number of policy makers, so it is necessary to proceed with a quantitative survey of a larger number of individuals using a questionnaire in order to develop a more holistic picture of the legal information environment within the two pilot countries, and then in other countries with different legal systems and traditions. Furthermore, it is necessary to implement the novel legal information services identified in our study, and then evaluate them, and possibly improve and extend them.

References

1. Lugo-Gil, J., Jean-Baptiste, D., Jaramillo, L.F.: Use of Evidence to Drive Decision-Making in Government. Math. Policy Res. (2019). https://www.mathematica.org/-/media/publications/pdfs/education/2019/useofevidenceindecisionmaking.pdf
2. Kamateri, E., et al.: A comparative analysis of tools and technologies for policy making. In: Janssen, M., Wimmer, Maria A., Deljoo, A. (eds.) Policy Practice and Digital Science. PAIT, vol. 10, pp. 125–156. Springer, Cham (2015). https://doi.org/10.1007/978-3-319-12784-2_7
3. ManyLaws Consortium: Deliverable 1.1: Report on the Assessment of Existing Tools, DSIs, and Data Infrastructures (2019)
4. Arnott, D., Pervan, G., O'Donnell, P., Dodson, G.: An analysis of decision support systems research: preliminary results. In: Proceedings of the 2004 IFIP International Conference on Decision Support Systems, pp. 25–37 (2004). [full citation unavailable]
5. Phillips-Wren, G., Jain, L.: Artificial intelligence for decision making. In: Gabrys, B., Howlett, R.J., Jain, L.C. (eds.) KES 2006. LNCS (LNAI), vol. 4252, pp. 531–536. Springer, Heidelberg (2006). https://doi.org/10.1007/11893004_69
6. Arnott, D., Pervan, G.: Eight key issues for the decision support systems discipline. Decis. Support Syst. 44(3), 657–672 (2008)
7. Sabatier, P.: Theories of the Policy Process. Routledge, New York (2019)
8. Jann, W., Wegrich, K.: Theories of the policy cycle. In: Fischer, F., Miller, G.J. (eds.) Handbook of Public Policy Analysis, pp. 69–88. Routledge, New York (2017)
9. Power, D.J.: Decision Support Systems: Concepts and Resources for Managers. Greenwood Publishing Group, Westport (2002)
10. Erdelez, S., O'Hare, S.: Legal informatics: application of information technology in law. Ann. Rev. Inf. Sci. Technol. 32, 367–402 (1997)
11. Sartor, G., Francesconi, E.: Legal informatics and legal concepts. In: Eurovoc Conference – 18–19 November 2010, Luxembourg (2010)
12. Hornsby, W.: Improving the delivery of affordable legal services through the internet: a blueprint for the shift to a digital paradigm (1999)
13. Byrd, O: Legal Analytics vs. Legal Research: What's the Difference?. Law Technology Today, 12 June 2017. https://www.lawtechnologytoday.org/2017/06/legal-analytics-vs-legal-research/
14. Ashley, K.D.: Artificial Intelligence and Legal Analytics: New Tools for Law Practice in the Digital Age. Cambridge University Press, Cambridge (2017)
15. Moens, M.-F.: Innovative techniques for legal text retrieval. Artif. Intell. Law 9(1), 29–57 (2001)
16. Casanovas, P., Palmirani, M., Peroni, S., Van Engers, T., Vitali, F.: Semantic web for the legal domain: the next step. Semantic Web 7(3), 213–227 (2016)
17. Schweighofer, E.: Semantic indexing of legal documents. In: Francesconi, E., Montemagni, S., Peters, W., Tiscornia, D. (eds.) Semantic Processing of Legal Texts. LNCS (LNAI), vol. 6036, pp. 157–169. Springer, Heidelberg (2010). https://doi.org/10.1007/978-3-642-12837-0_9
18. Otike, J.: Legal information needs of the general public. Libr. Rev. 46(1), 28–33 (1997)
19. Otike, J., Matthews, G.: Legal information needs of lawyers in Kenya: a case study. Libr. Manag. 21(5), 241–251 (2000)
20. Peoples, L.F.: Testing the limits of Westlaw next. Legal Refer. Serv. Q. 31(2), 125–149 (2012)
21. Bhardwaj, R.K., Margam, M.: Online legal information system for Indian environment: a user's perspectives. Libr. Rev. 65(8/9), 593–624 (2016)
22. Bhatt, A.A.: Information needs, perceptions and quests of law faculty in the digital era. Electr. Libr. 32(5), 659–669 (2014)

23. Bhardwaj, R.J.: Development of online legal information system: lawyers' perceptions. J. Libr. Inf. Technol. **39**(2), 131–139 (2019)
24. Van Lamsweerde, A.: Goal-oriented requirements engineering: a guided tour. In: Proceedings - Fifth IEEE International Symposium on Requirements Engineering, pp. 249–262. IEEE Press (2001)
25. Chamberlain, S., Sharp, H., Maiden, N.: Towards a Framework for Integrating Agile Development and User-Centred Design. In: Abrahamsson, P., Marchesi, M., Succi, G. (eds.) XP 2006. LNCS, vol. 4044, pp. 143–153. Springer, Heidelberg (2006). https://doi.org/10.1007/11774129_15
26. Collier, K.: Agile Analytics: a Value-Driven Approach to Business Intelligence and Data Warehousing. Addison-Wesley, Boston (2012)
27. Wiegers, K., Beatty, J.: Software Requirements. Pearson Education, Harlow, UK (2013)
28. Zowghi, D., Coulin, C.: Requirements elicitation: a survey of techniques, approaches, and tools. In: Aurum, A., Wohlin, C. (eds.) Engineering and Managing Software Requirements, pp. 19–46. Springer, Heidelberg (2005). https://doi.org/10.1007/3-540-28244-0_2
29. Paetsch, F., Eberlein, A., Maurer, F: Requirements engineering and agile software development. In Proceedings - Twelfth IEEE International Workshops on Enabling Technologies: Infrastructure for Collaborative Enterprises, pp. 308–313, WET ICE 2003. IEEE Press (2003)
30. Hennik, M., Hutter, I., Bailey, A.: Qualitative Research Methods. SAGE Publications, London (2011)
31. Yin, R.K.: Qualitative Research from Start to Finish. The Guilford Press, New York (2011)
32. Kumar. R: Research Methodology. A Step-by-Step Guide for Beginners, Fourth edn. SAGE Publications, London, UK (2014)
33. Lachana, Z., Loutsaris, M.A., Alexopoulos, C., Charalabidis, Y.: Automated analysis and interrelation of legal elements based on text mining. Int. J. E-Serv. Mobile Appl. (IJESMA) **12**(2), 79–96 (2020)
34. Loutsaris, M., Androutsopoulou, A., Charalabidis, Y.:. EU-wide legal text mining using big data processing infrastructures. In: 12th Mediterranean Conference on Information Systems (MCIS 2018) (2018)

Technology Mediated Citizenship: What Can We Learn from Library Practices

Mariana S. Gustafsson(✉) ⓘ, Elin Wihlborg ⓘ, and Johanna Sefyrin ⓘ

Department Management and Engineering IEI, Linköping University, 581 83 Linköping, Sweden
mariana.s.gustafsson@liu.se

Abstract. Advanced digital societies in democratic societies are conceived to be sustained by informed, active and responsible citizens. While internet and information technologies are both hailed for their empowering potential for the citizens to express their civic and political rights, they also pose considerable literacy and usage challenges, and thus can raise exclusionary thresholds for these same aspirations. Digital skills and information literacy as preconditions for tapping into such technology potential, can thus affect the way citizenship is practiced and conceived by the members of society. Based on an extensive field study at Swedish libraries practices with helping and educating clients with a wide diversity of questions relating to digital technologies and e-services, we examine both empirically and conceptually how citizenship is practiced in an advanced digital society, in a universal welfare state. The analysis focused on citizenship practices in daily activities when technologies mediate participation and interaction among the public, civic and market actors. The conclusions contribute to the conceptualization of citizenship act and agency and elaborates on citizenship as a performative process.

Keywords: Digital citizenship · Public digital services · Agency · Library

1 Background and Research Problem

In advanced digital societies, such as the in the Scandinavian countries, it is the responsibility of the 'active and informed citizen' to manage daily needs and activities, by accessing public services, communicating with authorities and businesses, or engaging in social or political acts [1]. These practices can be highly empowering and effective for the individual person. But an important precondition for empowerment to happen, she needs to be knowledgeable and skillful to use an array of different digital technologies that are mediating pretty much every relation and service in society [2]. For individual citizens to fulfil these requirements, in the current process of a swift digitalisation of public societal services, this is not easy, but requires various forms of support [3, 4]. There are policy ambitions to promote increased digitalisation and call for harnessing of digitalisation opportunities for economic growth and citizen well-being [2, 5–7]. 'People must have the opportunity to develop personally, to choose freely and safely, to engage in society, regardless of their age, gender or professional background' the European Commission writes in a recent communication [5]. Furthermore, they state: 'Citizens should

© IFIP International Federation for Information Processing 2020
Published by Springer Nature Switzerland AG 2020
S. Hofmann et al. (Eds.): ePart 2020, LNCS 12220, pp. 109–120, 2020.
https://doi.org/10.1007/978-3-030-58141-1_9

be empowered to make better decisions based on insights gleaned from non-personal data', thus calling for technologies that make a difference and work for people in their daily lives [5].

OECD calls for immediacy of policies that target digital literacy for effective use of technologies, and emphasize that these shall: 'empower people with the mix of skills needed to succeed, improve social protection to ensure no one is left behind' [8]. While finding proved effects of digitalisation on human productivity and accessibility to knowledge [7], they stress the risks of disinformation, insecurity and the digital divides that are inherent to the process of transformation in society [8]. Normative analyses have depicted the good citizenship implied in being an informed participant in democratic practices [9], while digital divide research showed that digital technologies empowered those already politically engaged and highly educated [3, 4].

The case of Sweden should be understood as an advanced and rather digitalized welfare state, rather than a universal welfare state. In this context we include in the concept of citizenship not only the right to vote (political citizenship), but also social, economic and civic engagement [10]. In this study, we focus on citizenship from a performative perspective, that involves what individuals actually do when they live in society, in their daily lives - solving mundane problems, fulfilling their different needs - civic, political, educational, financial. As Hintz, Dencik [11] clarify, participation in society is conditioned by receiving of citizen status, in contrast to enacting citizenship through engagement in social and political activities. In advanced information societies these activities are often digitalized, something which brings to the fore how digital access and skills condition the performing of citizenship (van Deursen & van Dijk, 2018). Swedish research shows that digital diversity involves always exclusionary potential and that citizenship should be examined as an entanglement of human and technology relations [12–15].

Libraries present valuable fora used increasingly by citizens to learn about and get help with digital technologies. The library as an institution is fundamental for the lively, engaged, inclusive and rooted democracy [16, 17]. The public libraries play a central function in the building of democratic and inclusive local communities, being increasingly relied upon by governments to deliver access and support for e-services [18]. In particular local public libraries have played a crucial role for deliberation, literacy and democratic inclusion during the building of the Scandinavian welfare states [19].

The Library Act in Sweden stipulates today that every municipality shall have a local library open for every citizen and adapted to their needs [20]. Public libraries are managed under the municipalities in Sweden and they are currently developing their organizations and services to meet the new and increasing demands on digital information and e-services. Eight out of ten libraries in Sweden are currently offering services targeting citizens' needs for digital information and services [21]. Through the libraries, citizens are supposed to get improved access to information, culture and values – which are preconditions for informed, active and engaged citizens in the civic realm. By providing access and qualified support to all citizens, the libraries are expected to promote access to information and knowledge resources for all individuals in society regardless of their economic and social resources. Hence, libraries and library employees work to support citizens' everyday activities in terms of digitalized relations with authorities and other organizations, as well as private matters,. In these terms the library employees become mediators and enablers of citizenship agency.

On this background, this paper will discuss how digitalization affects citizenship as performative enactment, viewed through the lens of Swedish library employees and their practices of supporting visitors with questions relating to access, understanding and acting upon digital services, digital information and technologies. The focus is the image of citizenship which emerges in the stories told and the observations of library practices to provide support for the visitors. These visitors come to the library because they need help with enacting their rights and obligations as citizens. Thus, citizens who are invoked in the empirical material is a limited group of citizens in different vulnerable positions due to lack of knowledge and/or ability to use information technologies, rather than representative for the whole population. Our main argument is that through digital mediation of social activities, the boundaries of what individuals can do in the frame of their citizen rights, responsibilities and duties are shifting depending on how they manage digital technologies and thereby digitalization re-frames the meaning of citizenship.

1.1 The Aim and the Research Questions

In this paper we aim to explore practices of citizenship in an advanced digital society as they are supported in library practices. Based on our findings and analyses we aim to open for a discussion on re-assessing the meaning of citizenship when its practicing is mediated by digital technologies. To pursue this aim, the paper will focus on three research questions:

- How is citizenship practiced in daily life activities through digital technologies?
- How do digital technologies affect the practice of citizenship and how are they supported by the library staff?
- What implications do technology mediated citizenship practices have upon citizenship acts and citizenship agency?

2 Literature Insights and Theoretical Framework

Digital citizenship has been described in terms of the ability of the individuals to participate in society through access and use of digital technologies as a critical medium for 'individual expression, democratization, economic opportunity, community and education' [22, 23]. The term is not new, it emerged at the same time as Internet became widely accessible for the public. This development resulted in a reflection of – and a challenge to rights, obligations and freedoms in the physical polities – democratic or authoritarian alike.

More recently, when digitalisation has permeated the depths of both public and private spheres - digital literacy, in addition to government knowledge is to drive the ability to participate online in society and politics [24]. Building on different literacies and technology affordances, the individuals engage in activities of 'becoming' digital citizens, by negotiating new ways of living their rights and freedoms [25, 26]. Critical analyses on digital citizenship from a governing perspective argue that through the popular education and the lifelong learning ideal, policies work to re-include citizens in a society that they already were part of, but were excluded by computerization [27].

2.1   Performative Citizenship in a Sociotechnical Landscape

When access and use of public services is increasingly digital, as well as online partic-ipation, deliberation and interaction with elected politicians and public servants, when digital infrastructure for e-legitimation and signature is systemically built – the institu-tional arrangements for democratic citizenship should be considered as socio-technical arrangements [28–31]. Consequently, there is a need to address these arrangements that make up the digital citizenship.

Current digital infrastructure in public sector that requires to perform digital acts can be compared with Winner [32] analysis of Moser bridges in '20s New York, as well as Chandler and Hikino [33] studies of large scale energy technology infrastructure and their early arguments about the political properties – intrinsic or by design, of technologies. The analogy in the citizenship case is to reflect upon what information technologies and digital (and automated) infrastructures in public services require or condition in terms of practicing citizenship acts and how human agency is affected by these.

2.2   Digital Citizenship as Performative Enactment

Studies of citizenship as practice - 'the doing of citizenship' – draw on theories of performativity that seek to understand how people manifest their citizenship through their activities [25, 34, 35] while claiming rights and implementing responsibilities [36]. Citizenship as practice comprise individuals' decisions and actions when claiming rights and implementing responsibilities as members of society. The practice should be seen in relation to the different statuses a person can have, where the citizenship establishes the belonging of the individual to a nation state, their legal and political regimes and entitlement to welfare. By acquiring the status of 'citizen', the person acquires a legal identity and a subjectivity in the frame of the national jurisdiction, with full rights and responsibilities towards the national state.

However, not all members in a society are 'citizens', as for example persons with rights to work and study, persons with residence rights, refugees or asylum seekers. Depending on these statuses, these people will have more or less limited access to rights, responsibilities and welfare services and thus their practices will involve differ-ent activities [37, 38]. In these terms the agency associated with citizenship is always conditioned, circumscribed by a number of regulations.

2.3   Citizen Acts and Citizen Agency

A performative perspective of citizenship will thus have 'citizen acts' and 'citizen agency' among the main units of analysis [35]. A citizen act is here broadly defined as intentional actions of individual subjects to engage with society [35]. Isin [35] pro-posed to shift the focus from the institution of citizenship and the citizen as an individual actor to acts of citizenship. Isin defined acts of citizenship as *individual deeds that rup-ture social-historical patterns*'. According to Isin, acts are not passively given, nor are they coming from a natural order. Citizenship acts are not simply the exercise of rights and obligations, '*as if these neutral forms of individual choice could be sanctioned outside multiple networks of authority'..., such practices like voting, paying taxes or learning languages appear passive and one-sided in mass democracies, whereas acts of citizenship break with repetition of the same...'* [35]. Citizenship shall thus also include acts of solving daily needs.

In a digital society, many of such citizen acts will be mediated by digital technologies, which will have an effect upon how citizens perform more advanced activities in society: how they live their rights, freedoms and obligations. How knowledgeable citizens are about their living conditions, how able they are to fulfill their daily needs and act upon them using technologies, will have effects upon their ability to participate in society, politically, socially and economically, in a more informed and timely manner. We argue that if a person has difficulties to act upon her daily needs by being restrained by technology, she will also be limited in her ability to engage in more advanced activities.

Along with rights and responsibilities granted by formal citizenship status - digital literacy, technology access and the abilities of the person to use such technologies will make up an important part of her citizenship agency. Citizen agency will thus consist of the ability of the person to perform citizen acts to fulfill the individual's social, political, cultural and financial needs. Importantly, citizenship agency is relational as it builds abilities based on the relations that the individual cultivates with technologies, authorities, and other supporting or mediating actors. Thus, practicing citizenship by using digital technologies daily becomes an important medium through which citizens enact their role in society [11]. Daily activities that involve purposefully using Internet to search for, access and use digital platforms of governmental authorities, public and private services providers - make up the agency with which the person performs and positions herself as a citizen in society. Such an agency builds on knowledge about the services and their providers, literacy of rights and obligations, the experience of solving problems through digital and other technologies and the relations with other members in the community. However, when the person lacks literacy, other actors supporting or mediating knowledge become important in building and sustaining citizenship agency, which is the case of library employees in this study.

3 Method

This study follows the path of 'library studies' and builds on our interest to follow the process of advancing digitalization of society and the implications for citizens' participation in democratic practices [12, 39]. The public library as an institution is framed as a democracy arena that works for broad folk literacy and digital inclusions [40–42]. The study focused on library activities occurring at a main public library in a medium sized municipality in Sweden, at one of its local branches in a housing area and at the regional library program for Introduction of asylum seekers to society, where social communicators work.

Acts of citizenship and agency were studied through the stories of the library employees, and in our observations at the library information desk. Through these main sources we learned about the visitors' individual needs and challenges when attempting to perform citizenship acts. These visitors can be understood as a vulnerable group of citizens, rather than representative of all Swedish citizens. Compared to the average in Sweden, the citizens in this municipality had a slightly lower level of education, lower level of income, and shorter average lifespan [43]. A relatively high number of immigrants lived in the municipality, which also showed in their attendance of the libraries in focus.

The study was designed as a qualitative, interpretive study with included elements of ethnographic studies. Besides documentary information, the empirical material was collected through seven semi-structured interviews, about an hour in length, with library employees and managers (all were librarians), 29 documented observation visits during daily activities at the library information desk, IT-tutorials and courses, events such e-Citizen week, All Digital Week, and two focus groups with social communicators. The observations range from one to several hours in length, and the focus groups comprised two hours each.

This material was corroborated with our empirical findings from our previous library studies [13, 39]. This interpretive analysis employed an abductive procedure and connected the concepts of 'citizenship acts', 'digital acts' and 'agency' to the empirical content, which was in its turn ground for assessing the theoretical concepts [44, 45]. Our interest lies in both explaining the empirical questions of citizenship practices and hoping that these findings would contribute to refine theory of citizenship. The material was coded in NVIVO, in this case by focusing on citizenship. The codes 'need', 'knowledge', 'technology', 'support', 'challenge' were included in the analysis, but also grounded theory approach allowing for themes such as 'concern', 'boundaries', 'responsibility' to emerge from the material.

4   Findings from Library Practices

To embed the discussion in practical situations, we will use critical situations as we have identified in the field studies that illustrate examples of activities mediated by digital technologies, and later to relate them to acts of citizenship.

4.1   Daily Digital Acts that Make the Practice of Citizenship

As we argued above, members of society practice their rights and responsibilities daily – in more or less obvious forms and based on a diversity of needs that arise from lived experiences. Confirming earlier studies, we find that library visitors increasingly address questions and ask for assistance to manage access and exchange of information with authorities in the public and private sector. It is through the lens of their challenges that we shall understand their citizen acts and their agency in the digital society.

Printing papers or digitizing paper records present the most popular kind of assistance at the library: activity reports for unemployment benefits, monthly account statement and receipts for municipality income support services, records asked by banking services. Not so seldom, the person who is not able to manage the entire communication via e-services, chooses to present them on paper. So far some of these authorities still accept papers. We observed and got confirmed by the interviewed staff at the branch library that in the areas inhabited by immigrants, non-speakers of Swedish and socially vulnerable households, such questions and assistance is much more frequent than at the central library. Some more examples follow on public transportation, when buses are not accepting cash or paper tickets:

Two young women asking for help to print bus tickets QR code, when staff 2, wonders why she cannot just show it on her mobile. It turns out the women's mobile does not have internet connection and the women was unsure whether she could use her QR-app to show the code to the ticket scanner. She prints a huge QR-code on paper and leaves (Obsr. Branch 7, Ref 1).

One of the visitors turned out to have a smartphone without internet connection, which hindered her to handle the ticket app and use the ticket scanner on the bus. A similar case, almost anecdotal, occurred when another library visitor had two different mobiles which he could not use (ex. google maps) to find the address and the route to the specific store he needed. Pursuing without hinder such elementary acts will facilitate or sometimes pre-condition the persons contacts with the authorities, the employers or health care. A house rental situation was observed as follows:

An older lady needs help to post an ad on Internet about renting her apartment: "Where would you like to place your ad?", she is asked. She replied "I don't know, anywhere. I don't know where to post ads. I don't have my own computer". She is curious about computers, but afraid to become dependent on them, she admits. After explaining her intention, she gets the advice to contact the local rental housing company. But she explained that she had tried but has not got any help. Finally, the alternative was suggested to post the ad in the local newspaper, but for that she needed to have an email account. (Obsr. Main 2, Ref 1).

Here again, we witness several elementary acts that the person needs to know and manage digitally. Even when an alternative to use the print newspaper, it turns out she needed to mail them her request online, for which she needed to have an email account and know the password for login. Knowing about the service, knowing the language is in many cases not enough anymore. Handling logins to email, passwords, mobiles, websites and computers become mediators of elementary digital acts of the citizen.

4.2 Digital Acts and Challenges Connecting to Welfare Services

Our field studies suggest that more advanced activities, like accessing and using public e-services to solve daily needs involve more digital acts and higher citizenship agency abilities. To recall, her agency will thus be her ability to perform citizen acts based on her knowledge and understanding of the services, knowing of her rights and responsibilities entitling her to social, cultural, and political benefits, but also her relation with the respective authorities and communication abilities through digital technologies.

A specific case that illustrates a challenge of agency concerns the decision of the local public schools in to introduce paper free communication policies. Certain parents with daycare or school children, had difficulties communicating with the schools through basic digital means such as emails or through the municipality school platform. These parents needed much more assistance to use the digital platforms at the transmit the information about the pupil, but more often they needed support when the services did not function based on wrong or missing information. The observation below describes a typical situation occurring at the library:

A woman around 40 y.o. approaches the library reception. She tells the library staff that since her children's school recently has become paper-free and she needed help to report special diet for one of her children. The woman is annoyed. Staff 1 replies that [the municipal] contact centers will attend libraries during specific hours to assist parents with such issues. The woman admits she can't attend during those hours. She replies: "why should it be so damn hard and take such a damn time [for the staff to help her]". The class teacher and the school administration advised her to use the library help desk for the purpose. (Obsr. Branch 10, Ref 2)

Another common support activity is counseling on IT problems, both on spot when the questions are posed in the reception and in booked sessions, as illustrated by the following examples:

Woman, 50 years old, who has recently become a custodian needs to buy a new computer to be able to manage the custodee's economy. [Earlier] she was hesitant to use new computers, but now as she needed to use Internet banking, she will need a more secure computer. She asks the staff for advice on the type of computer, the software and the broadband security. She seems to know many of the answers but asks to get confirmation (Obsr. Main 1, Ref 1).

Or, missing the communication with the authorities, as witnessed by one of the librarians:

[it's] various contacts with authorities, like the National Insurance Office, The Swedish Employment Service, this way you should fill in an activity report. You shall fill in time reports, [ed. asking himself] "how should I do? what should I do?" My husband just received a payment from the unemployment fund, several months after he had applied and he did not understand how it worked at all and he had not seen that he had a message in his inbox in the system (Interview Librarian 2).

And the list of such queries is long, as all the interviewed staff confirmed: activity reports for social services as bank account statements, check ins to flights or printing. Many of them have difficulties understanding the Swedish language on the websites or computer programs, as discussed in interviews and seen during observations.

So, what do these cases have in common? In each of these examples, we see persons who have challenges to act upon their rights to use the e-services, both in public and in private sector. For them to use most of the services (banks, shops, schools, authorities), they need to access the information, understand it and act upon it to fulfill a diversity of needs arising in their daily life. A they seem to have limited agency in daily activities, these persons will experience more exclusions and difficulties to reach out. Their citizenship agency is increasingly depending on support and assistance with different digital technologies. We argue that such acts present elementary citizenship acts that underly more advanced acts and make up for an autonomous citizen's agency. A person's integration in the labor market, her balance of work-life activities, her social or political affordances for engagement and influence in society is now mediated by technologies and conditioned by her information literacy.

When a library visitor turns to the library information desk with her questions – they usually seem as rather simple questions – 'please help me to print my bank statement', 'I can't log in to the employment agency's website', all related to some kind of device and with the purpose of solving an issue with the authorities or banks. For certain clients – usually old, immigrants or with functional disabilities, but not only – these are not easy tasks. These mundane tasks of reporting to the insurance agency, or activity reporting to the social assistance services, or booking a visit to the doctor, or checking out the balance on the bank account – are difficult if not impossible for them to solve independently through digital systems.

Our study finds that the library staff experience this at the counter and in IT-guidance meetings daily. The practice is similar for the society communicators who work with asylum seekers: what seems to be a very basic task for most of the clients – it may turn a rather difficult challenge for the certain individuals. Such seemingly simple tasks pursued by the client should be seen as assemblages of entangled questions (what do I need to do in order to solve my problem), information (what do I need to know), devices (why can't I log in to this computer or webpage, why is this app not opening) and concerns (will I ever get employed, will I get may income by the end of this month), requirements (of a personal security number, passwords) and signatures (e-ID).

5 Discussion and Conclusions

This study focused on the doing of citizenship in daily practices in the context of an advanced welfare society and concerned a limited group of citizens who were in different vulnerable positions. Based on the study of this particular group we argue that along with rights and responsibilities granted by formal citizenship status - digital literacy, technology access and the abilities of the person to use such technologies will make up an important part of her citizenship agency. Her citizen agency is proven in practice and builds on knowledge about the services and their providers, literacy of rights and obligations, the experience of solving problems through digital and other technologies and the relations with other members and authorities in the community. Such agency, based on Isin and Ruppert [46] argument, makes up the citizen's role and position in society, serving as claims to the right to act 'freely' in both digital environments and physical environments [11].

This study shows that the activity of citizenship involves an entanglement of artifacts (technology), people and concerns, information, and knowledge. The agency of citizenship is made up of such entanglements of people with authorities, technology, and information. It points at the importance of studying such entanglements to understand how citizenship evolves when practiced through digital acts and mediated by technology.

In daily situations when the technology does not work or is not available, or the information available to the person is limited or misunderstood - the agency for citizenship is also limited and that results in hindering her participation in society, her relationship with the authorities, and with other community actors. With such limited agency, the person will have a limited de facto access to the benefits of the digital society, will experience more exclusion and will be less able to act upon her social and political rights, responsibilities, and economic opportunities. Such examples of limited agency for citizenship are abounding in library practices. The library staff in such cases are supporting to restore and untangle such assemblages.

However, while they play an important supporting role, the citizen's autonomy and the scope of her opportunities to engage in society will be affected. In certain cases, when the person will acquire literacy and skills, they will empower her agency, while in other cases – when the citizen becomes dependent on such support, it will have opposite effects. Such effects of different actors and technologies upon citizenship agency should be carefully studied and need further research. Finally, a re-assessment of institutional arrangements for citizenship in information societies, increasingly mediated by technologies is critical in order to understand how citizenship agency evolves and how these are negotiated to reflect the actual challenges and conditions for social and political engagement.

References

1. Eggers, T., Grages, C., Pfau-Effinger, B.: Self-responsibility of the "active social citizen": different types of the policy concept of "active social citizenship" in different types of welfare states. Am. Behav. Sci. **63**(1), 43–64 (2019)
2. van Laar, E., et al.: The relation between 21st-century skills and digital skills: a systematic literature review. Comput. Hum. Behav. **72**(1), 577–588 (2017)
3. van Deursen, A.J., van Dijk, J.A.: The first-level digital divide shifts from inequalities in physical access to inequalities in material access. New Media Soc. **21**(2), 354–375 (2019)
4. Scheerder, A., van Deursen, A., van Dijk, J.: Determinants of Internet skills, uses and outcomes A systematic review of the second- and third-level digital divide. Telematics Inform. **34**(8), 1607–1624 (2017)
5. European Commission: Shaping Europe's Digital Future (2020)
6. Regeringskansliet: För ett hållbart digitaliserat Sverige – en digitaliseringsstrategi, Näringsdepartementet. Stockholm (2017)
7. OECD: How's Life in the Digital Age?: Opportunities and Risks of the Digital Transformation for People's Well-Being, OECD Publishing, Paris (2019)
8. OECD: Going Digital: Shaping Policies, Improving Lives, OECD Publishing, Paris (2019)
9. Shelley, I.I., et al.: Lost in cyberspace: barriers to bridging the digital divide in e-politics. Int. J. Internet Enterp. Manage. **4**(3), 228–243 (2006)
10. Svallfors, S.: Class, attitudes and the Welfare State: Sweden in comparative perspective. Soc. Policy Adm. **38**(2), 119–138 (2004)
11. Hintz, A., Dencik, L., Wahl-Jorgensen, K.: Digital Citizenship in a Datafied Society. Polity Press, Cambridge (2019)
12. Sefyrin, J., Gustafsson, M.S., Wihlborg, E.: Addressing digital diversity in a digitalized society: ethics of care in a swedish library context. In: European Group for Public Administration (EGPA), Belfast (2019)
13. Gustafsson, M., Larsson, J., Wihlborg, E.: It is unbelievable how many come to us': a study on librarians' perspectives on digital inclusion in Sweden. In: The 15th Scandinavian Workshop on e-Government, Copenhagen, January 31–February 1 2018 (2018)
14. Gustafsson, M.S., Wihlborg, E.: 'It is always an individual assessment': a case study on challenges of automation of income support services. In: Lindgren, I., Janssen, M., Lee, H., Polini, A., Rodríguez Bolívar, M.P., Scholl, H.J., Tambouris, E. (eds.) EGOV 2019. LNCS, vol. 11685, pp. 45–56. Springer, Cham (2019). https://doi.org/10.1007/978-3-030-27325-5_4

15. Wihlborg, E., Gustafsson, M.S.: Automation of income support in the public social services: a case study of an innovation that is still struggling. In: Gråsjö, U., Bernhard, I., Karlsson, C. (eds.) Regional Innovation and Entrepreneurship Potentials - How to Unlock Them? Edward Elgar Publishing: Cheltenham (2021, forthcoming)

16. Bertot, J.C.: Community-based e-Government: libraries as e-Government partners and providers. In: Electronic Government: Proceedings of the 9th IFIP WG 8.5 International Conference, EGOV 2010, Lausanne, Switzerland (2010)

17. Palfrey, J.G.: Bibliotech: Why Libraries Matter More Than Ever in the Age of Google. Basic Books, A Member of the Perseus Books Group, New York (2013)

18. Jaeger, P.T., et al.: The intersection of public policy and public access: digital divides, digital literacy, digital inclusion, and public libraries. Public Libr. Q. **31**(1), 1–20 (2012)

19. Hedemark, Å.: Mötet mellan folkbibliotek och användare. Svensk biblioteksforskning **15**(1), 7 (2005)

20. SFS 2013:801, Bibliotekslag. Sveriges Riksdag (2013)

21. Norberg, I.: Insatser för digital kompetens på folkbiblioteken: En studie om folkbibliotekens arbete med digital delaktighet (2017)

22. Mossberger, K.: Toward digital citizenship: addressing inequality in the information age. In: Politics, A.C., Howard, P.N. (eds.) Routledge Handbook of Internet, pp. pp. 173–185. Routledge, London (2009)

23. Mossberger, K., Tolbert, C.J., McNeal, R.S.: Digital Citizenship: The Internet, Society, and Participation. MIT Press, Cambridge (2008). 221 p.

24. Lindgren, S.: Digital Media & Societ. SAGE Publications, Thousand Oaks (2017)

25. McCosker, A., Vivienne, S., Johns, A. (eds.): Negotiating Digital Citizenship: Control, Contest and Culture. Rowman & Littlefield International, Lanham (2016)

26. McCosker, A., Johns, A.: Contested publics: racist rants, bystander action and social media acts of citizenship. Media Int. Aust. **151**(1), 66–72 (2014)

27. Rahm, L., Fejes, A.: Popular education and the digital citizen: a genealogical analysis. Eur. J. Res. Educ. Learn. Adults **8**(1), 21–36 (2017)

28. Nafria, J.M.D., Cendon, J.A., Alonso, L.P.: Building up eParticipatory decision-making from the local to the global scale. Study case at the European Higher Education Area. Comput. Hum. Behav. **47**, 26–41 (2015)

29. Ingrams, A.: Mobile phones, smartphones, and the transformation of civic behavior through mobile information and connectivity. Gov. Inf. Q. **32**(4), 506–515 (2015)

30. Enggong, L., Whitworth, B.: Investigating personal and community factors in e-government: a citizen's perspective. In: 16th Pacific Asia Conference on Information Systems (PACIS 2012), Ho Chi Minh City, Vietnam (2012)

31. Geels, F.W.: Ontologies, socio-technical transitions (to sustainability), and the multi-level perspective. Res. Policy **39**(4), 495–510 (2010)

32. Winner, L.: Do artifacts have politics? Daedalus **109**(1), 121–136 (1980)

33. Chandler, A.D., Hikino, T.: Scale and Scope: The Dynamics Of Industrial Capitalism. Belknap Press, Cambridge (1990)

34. Isin, E.: Citizens Without Frontiers. Continuum, London (2012)

35. Isin, E.: Theorizing acts of citizenship. In: Isin, E.F., Nielsen, G.M. (eds.) Acts of Citizenship, pp. 15–43. Palgrave Macmillan, London (2008)

36. Zivi, K.: Making Rights Claims: A Practice of Democratic Citizenship. Oxford University Press, New York (2012)

37. Dryzek, J.S.: Deliberative Democracy and Beyond: Liberals, Critics, Contestations. Oxford University Press, Oxford (2000)

38. Fishkin, J.S.: When the People Speak Deliberative Democracy and Public Consultation. Oxford University Press, Oxford (2011)

39. Bernhard, I., et al.: A digital society for all?: meanings, practices and policies for digital diversity. In: 52nd Hawaii International Conference on System Sciences (HICSS-52), Hawaii, USA (2019)
40. Bertot, J.C.: Building digitally inclusive communities: the roles of public libraries in digital inclusion and development. In: 9th International Conference on Theory and Practice of Electronic Governance (ICEGOV 2015–2016). ACM, New York (2016)
41. McDermott, A.J., Bertot, J.C., Jaeger, P.T.: Digital inclusion and the affordable care act: public libraries, politics, policy, and enrollment in "Obamacare". Public Libr. Q. **34**(1), 1–22 (2015)
42. Bertot, J.C., Butler, B.S., Travis, D.M.: Local big data: the role of libraries in building community data infrastructures. In: Proceedings of the 15th Annual International Conference on Digital Government Research (dg.o 2014), Aguascalientes, Mexico (2014)
43. Rådet för främjande av kommunala analyser, Kolada: Den öppna och kostnadsfria databasen för kommuner och regioner (2020)
44. Alvesson, M., Sandberg, J.: Constructing Research Questions: Doing Interesting Research. SAGE, London (2013)
45. Alvesson, M., Kärreman, D.: Qualitative Research and Theory Development: Mystery as Method. Sage Publications, Thousand Oaks (2011)
46. Isin, E., Ruppert, E.: Digital citizenship and surveillancelcitizen Snowden. Int. J. Commun. (Online) **11**, 832–846 (2017)

eHealth in the Hood: Exploring Digital Participation in a Swedish Suburb

Karin Skill$^{(\boxtimes)}$ (iD) and Ahmed Kaharevic

The Department for Engineering and Management, Linköping University,
58183 Linköping, Sweden
`karin.skill@liu.se`

Abstract. In this paper we explore digital participation and inclusion in eHealth in a marginalized neighborhood, a suburb, in Sweden and present a survey method where face-to-face interviews in different languages are used. We also use statistics from a regional eHealth application, including data on doctor's visits, as a point of departure for our presentation and analysis of our data on digital participation, usage, and experiences of, and attitudes to digital technologies and services. Furthermore, we address the United Nations' call for disaggregated data on sustainable development and wide inclusion, which correlate to welfare policies at national, regional, and municipal levels and eHealth. We contribute by using a method to explore digital participation, eHealth literacy and attitudes among disadvantaged populations in among hard to survey groups by highlighting differences extracted from disaggregated data on age, ethno-national identification, mother tongue, occupation, and sex. We compare our results with a national survey on internet use, and data from a digital health app used by public sector.

Keywords: Digital participation · eHealth literacy · Disaggregated data · Suburb

1 Introduction: Why Surveying the Suburb?

As many welfare services are managed in digital channels, we need to understand how people participate and use digital health services, i.e. are included in digital society. eHealth has been among the areas investigated in studies of digital divide [1]. Research on eHealth and digital divide often discusses eHealth literacy among disadvantaged populations, like low income, the elderly, immigrant women or unemployed [2, 3]. eHealth literacy is about "the ability to seek, find, understand and appraise health information from electronic sources and apply the knowledge gained to addressing or solving a health problem" [4]. This literacy is like the model on digital divide, presented by van Dijk [1], where motivation, access, competence, and usage are aspects of digital inclusion. Digital participation is often explored with surveys [1, 7]. We know little about digital participation among groups considered hard to survey (that they seldom participate in surveys), like residents in Swedish suburbs [6].

Digital inclusion and participation are central in a democratic welfare state and are also a prerequisite to implement the United Nations Agenda 2030 for transformation

© IFIP International Federation for Information Processing 2020
Published by Springer Nature Switzerland AG 2020
S. Hofmann et al. (Eds.): ePart 2020, LNCS 12220, pp. 121–132, 2020.
https://doi.org/10.1007/978-3-030-58141-1_10

with the seventeen accompanying sustainable development goals (SDGs), including a general ambition to leave no one behind [8]. The UN asks for disaggregated statistical data on progress towards the goals, something that Statistics Sweden aim at contributing [9].

1.1 Previous Studies of eHealth, Digital Participation, and Literacy

Previous studies have pointed out that public sector is expected to implement digital solutions to cut costs, and at the same time citizens are expected to make health appointments, find information, and monitor their health in digital channels [2–4, 28]. There are literally thousands of digital applications for diagnosis and care of illnesses, and patients are encouraged to make decisions, book appointments, and follow their cases in digital channels. However, citizens who lack digital literacy may be excluded and experience what Gann calls digital health inequality [2], an aspect of the digital divide. Furthermore, groups of people who experience illness tend to be less digitally competent and less online, which is a challenge for digital inclusion [2]. Digital exclusion seems to be related to social exclusion, aging population, and access to technology or infrastructure [1] and even language [2]. The health centers are collecting data on customer satisfaction through surveys, for example the national patient survey [11]. However, response rates are low in hard to survey groups like residents in Swedish suburbs [6, 12], and there is a lack of feedback from surveys on customer satisfaction [11, 13]. When groups in a population do not participate in surveys it is difficult to know what their opinions and attitudes are. To reap the benefits expected from digitalization, as expressed above, inhabitants need to trust digital services and not the least, use them.

1.2 Aim and Research Questions

The aim of this paper is to explore digital participation around eHealth with a specific survey method in a Swedish suburb considered hard to survey. The research questions are: How do residents use digital technologies and services related to eHealth? What attitudes do residents express towards digital services?

The paper proceeds as follows. First, we motivate the study and give background information about the neighborhood. We describe the application Digital Health Center and data on who uses it. Then we present the survey method and assumptions related to the design of the survey. We compare our results with the nationwide survey Svenskarna och Internet, (SoI) performed by Internetstiftelsen [7]. Last, we present results and conclusions on attitudes and practices related to eHealth in the suburb, the hood.

2 Background

Inclusion and participation are central to eHealth, from the ambitions at the UN for sustainable development [8], to Swedish welfare policies [14, 15]. As services are digitalized the local authorities become responsible for taking care of inhabitants who lack digital competence. Initiatives for digital inclusion take place at libraries, citizen centers and study organizations [18, 19]. Lately, citizen centers in Linköping have been reorganized to care only for digital services provided by the municipality (Kontakt Linköping), which has implied that service for national authorities (i.e. Swedish Public Employment Service, Social Insurance Agency) and their digital services are coordinated elsewhere. The same goes for services provided by the regional authorities such as health services including eHealth. At the local health center in the neighborhood in focus in this paper, Skäggetorp, which is in Linköping, staff considers that many patients in the area do not comprehend Swedish well enough to complete the survey for customer satisfaction, and do not have access to computers where the survey is available in different languages, thus results from the survey are not perceived as fair [13]. When comparing the response rate with other areas in the region the response rate in Skäggetorp is more than twice as low [13]. This requirement to complete surveys directs attention to what can be perceived as good "digitally active" care takers who use digital devices. In a conversation with medical staff at Skäggetorp health center within this study, they emphasized that their impression is that the developers of digital services, like the app Digital Health Center do not comprehend that patients/residents in Skäggetorp need service through other channels. We need to attend to this indication that people use the Internet and digital services in diverse ways.

2.1 Skäggetorp: Description of a Marginalized Neighborhood

Skäggetorp is a marginalized neighborhood. The Police calls it particularly vulnerable, due to the influence of criminal activities. But this way of characterizing the area and its residents is stigmatizing, and "förorten" i.e. "suburb" is a term that many inhabitants prefer, according to studies in similar areas [6]. Indeed, there had recently been shootings in the streets when we performed the study. Yet, we were almost exclusively warmly welcome when we moved around in the area and residents talked about it as their home.

The population is characterized by high numbers of immigrants and there are many different languages spoken. In Table 1 statistics about different areas of Linköping municipality are compared to Skäggetorp.

Table 1. Comparison of characteristics in different areas of Linköping municipality [21]

	Inhabitants November 2019	Proportion not born in Sweden 2019	Disposable average household income (SEK) 2017	Proportion living on income support 2018
Municipality	162 984	18%	354 900	3,4%
Skäggetorp	10 313	56%	250 000	18,0%
Inner city	11 334	15%	327 000	1,8%

2.2 The App Digital Health Center as an Example of eHealth

A region is the Swedish authority that is responsible for organizing health care. Since 2018 the Region of Östergötland, where Skäggetorp is located, offers video appointments through an application (app) called "Digitala Vårdcentralen" (the Digital Health Center). The app is framed as making the health center "always close, wherever you are," and it is for administration and making appointments that do not require physical meetings, such as counseling, assessments, urgent prescription renewal, as well as physiotherapy. The app is part of the Primary Health center as in many Swedish regions, but there are also private sector alternatives. However, the difference between private and public services are not always clear to the users. To use the app a person must: 1. Download the app (from Google Play or App Store) on a smartphone or digital reader. The app asks for permission to use the device's camera and microphone 2. Find a date and time that fits 3. Make the appointment by using personal banking ID. The cost is 200 SEK and the same as when visiting the health center in person. For the meeting to start, the user logs on with bankID, a Swedish electronic identification. The check is sent to the address where the user is registered. The app is only provided in Swedish. Regional administrations attempt to cut costs with digital health visits in a similar manner as private companies. The cost of the digital visits supplied by private companies through apps, become part of the cost of the public sector [18]. This way digitalization of public sector is accelerated by developments in private sector [19].

2.3   Comparison with Data Compiled from the App Digital Health Center

Data from the Primary Health center in the Region of Östergötland, enable comparison with the health center in Skäggetorp. The number of doctor's visits in the whole region during February 2019 to January 2020 was 1 567 through the Digital Health Center, and out of them 2 were performed in Skäggetorp [17]. Skäggetorp is among the areas where least doctor's visits are made with the app. The amount of doctor's visits in Skäggetorp is very different in comparison to health centers in the center of towns like Motala with 122 visits, and central Linköping with 92 and 91 visits at the two different health centers [20]. The survey by Internetstiftelsen reports that 10% of the respondents use apps for doctor's visits, and 50% use eHealth services such as renewing medical receipts or reading personal medical records [7]. The low usage of the app in Skäggetorp is a challenge for eHealth.

Skäggetorp has 9 291 persons listed at the health center, while Kungsgatan in central Linköping has 14 036. Based on knowledge about the population who attend the different health centers mentioned above, in terms of average income, share of the population who was born outside of the Nordic countries, share of the population who live on income support, and employment there seem to be a connection between use of the Digital Health Center and above mentioned situation of the population. A similar pattern can be discerned from the data on conversational treatment administered via Internet, where the health centers in the center of Linköping have the highest numbers, while in Skäggetorp the numbers are considerably lower. The Skäggetorp health center has a high degree of accessibility by phone, 99% while Kungsgatan has 93% [17]. Age seems to be of relevance when comparing the amount of appointments done at different health centers – the higher share of people in the age groups 65 and above, the more appointments. Since central Linköping and Skäggetorp have a similar distribution of elderly, it is relevant to compare the number of digital appointments between them.

2.4   A Description of the Survey Method to Reach Hard to Survey Groups

The method proposed in this study is a survey technique where people are interviewed face-to-face or by answering questions by themselves on a digital reader/tablet, alternatively in special cases on a paper survey. The selection of respondents is spontaneous. Respondents are recruited by their household door or in public spaces and offered a small cash incentive of approximately 10 Euro for a local grocery store. The inspiration to use a cash check to increase response rates was from housing companies [6].

To participate the respondent should be adult, above 18 years of age, and live in Skäggetorp. Approximately 7 000 adult inhabitants live in Skäggetorp. Our goal was to ask 500 respondents, which we did, and we got a 65% response rate with 323 respondents. Some respondents denied participation due to the number of questions and time required; there were a maximum of 83 questions that took between 10 to 40 min or more for someone who needed help to understand the questions and the response alternatives, or wanted to shared experiences related to the questions. The latter is an added value of the method since the interviewer gets contextual information on digital participation about how the respondents reason about the questions and answers. The multilingual interview team could often solve language challenges. However, as has been pointed out in methodological literature, there is a risk of interviewer bias when performing face-to-face survey interviews [20].

2.5   Design of the Survey Questions and Analysis of Data

Many questions in our survey are from the nationwide survey of internet usage by Internetstiftelsen [7]. They remark on having problems reaching inhabitants who do not speak Swedish well [7], which was a motivation for our study and our multilingual team. The question about Internet use conditioned other questions about how and for what they use it, and thus people who answered that they do *not* use the Internet did not have to answer these. The use of bankID is an indicator for participation in Swedish digital welfare society and was central. Several questions are from Esaiasson's survey on trust and social cohesion [6]. Two questions about the Digital Health Center were added after conversations with the staff at the health center in Skäggetorp.

From an analytical perspective it is interesting to explore what kind of data people are willing to share when it comes to eHealth. The increase of eHealth has raised concerns for cybersecurity in the health sector [23]. When using a health app, including both private and public ones like the Digital Health Center, users must accept to share their data through their smartphone camera. The issue of surveillance has been raised in different contexts, and in our survey, we included questions from Internetstiftelsen's survey about this. Trust is a central aspect of attitude towards authorities and a dimension of social cohesion [6] and should be acknowledged when services are digitalized. We share descriptive statistics with some cross-tabulation [22].

2.6   Experiences of Using the Survey Method

The cash check distribution has been administered by a student consultancy firm, where students who speak Arabic, Somalian, and Kurdish were recruited. Even if the incentive was important for many, not the least to complete the survey with many questions, there were also some respondents who did not want the cash check.

We have been invited to organizations where local leaders and activists have helped to explain what the survey questions imply. From our meetings with representatives from local authorities and educational organizations, civic organizations, or job coaches we got insights into the way they fill the void of public offices as more and more services are digitalized, and all inhabitants do not comprehend them. They become digital coaches, but they also help with tricky civic activities like filling out a survey. We have worked in the area at different hours of the day all days of the week, even though we have been more active during daytime, when it is reasonable to believe that we encounter people who are at home with kids, elderly, students and people on sick leave, or people who work shifts. We noticed that young people came by in public spaces and asked if they could participate to "make 10 Euro", while this was not the case when we knocked on household doors. This insight is reflected in the high number of young respondents (90 respondents in the age of 18–25), and in the fact that the response rate differs between public spaces and organizations in comparison to household doors. Still, in Linköping, the share of people aged 18–25 is bigger amongst people born outside of Europe than people born in Sweden [21]. We did not collect personal data to comply with research ethics. The method is time consuming and complex to organize but rewarding in terms of knowledge about digital participation since it contributes with both quantitative and qualitative data.

Through the project we have met people who most likely would not have completed a survey if they had not been approached by an interviewer personally and/or an interviewer who speaks their mother tongue, and due to the cash check of course. But also, people who do not use the Internet and initially felt the study was not meant for them, participated after the interviewer explained that non-users could participate as well.

3   Results and Disaggregated Data from the Survey

We have met with a diversity of respondents in terms of age, sex, country of origin, literacy, mother tongue, occupation, education, digital competence, and usage. The number of respondents was 323 140 participated when we visited households and 193 when we attended public spaces and organizations. To count as possible respondent, the person must understand the purpose of the study, how the survey is performed, and that the participation is confidential and that we did not collect personal data. For 240 interviews we used the survey in Swedish (including orally translated interviews or interviews that were performed in several languages simultaneously with the help of the multilingual interviewing team), 30 used the Arabic, 22 the Somalian, 17 the Bosnian, and 13 the English survey.

Out of all respondents, 281 answered that they use the Internet, and 42 do not. This implies that 13% do not use the Internet. During the interviews we noticed how some have learned to use one single function on their smartphone, like an app for calls, but are not using any other apps, like bankID. Among those with low literacy, there are of course more difficulties with the use of all text based digital services.

Out of all the respondents 75% uses bankID, in comparison to 84% in Internetstiftelsen's survey [7]. 59% of our respondents feel decision-making is inclusive to a full, high or some extent. This question is from the Agenda 2030 for sustainable development [9]. When it comes to access to technology as van Dijk highlights [1], 81% of the 323 respondents has a smartphone, 16% does not and 3% does not know. 73% has a computer or a tablet, 26% does not, and 1% does not know. Following van Dijk's model, motivation is important apart from physical access. Attitude was explored with the question about feeling part of digital society.

In comparison with the survey by Internetstiftelsen [7] 9% answered No, not at all on the question expressed in Table 2 about feeling included in digital society. In our study 21% reported the same answer. This is among the more interesting differences between our study and theirs. In our survey, the share of respondents who reported not feeling included in digital society is further larger among women than men; 24% of females while 17% of the men reported No, not at all. This is disaggregated data.

Table 2. Do you feel included in digital society?

	Yes, completely	Yes, largely	Yes, but only a little	No, not at all	I don't know	Total
Number	72	80	72	67	32	323
%	22%	25%	22%	21%	10%	

3.1 Trust in Health Centers and Concerns About Cybersecurity

To be able to analyze the results about eHealth, we include the results about trust in the regular physical health center.

As seen in Table 3 younger respondents report lower trust in the health center, and reported level of trust raises with age, except in the age group 46–55, which is still higher than in the age group 18–25. The age group 56–65 reports the lowest trust, where 24% report 1 and 2, compared to only 7% in the age group 75+. A cross tabulation with gender shows that females report alternative 5 and 4 slightly more than males, and thus express higher trust.

Table 3. Level of trust in the health center per age groups (answer unknown is excluded)

Level of trust	18–25	26–35	36–45	46–55	56–65	55–75	75+	Total
5 and 4 (higher trust)	49%	58%	66%	73%	63%	72%	86%	62%
2 and 1 (lower trust)	20%	18%	22%	17%	24%	16%	7%	19%
Respondents per age group	90	67	58	30	30	32	15	323

Of the three largest ethnocultural/national groups in the survey, respondents who identify as Swedish report highest trust (alternatives 5 and 4) in the regular health center,

72%, while 53% of Syrians choose those alternatives, and 58% of the Somalians. Here we recognize that Swedish respondents were older than other groups. The number of respondents who identify as Syrian are considerably fewer than those who identify as Somalian and Swedish. When cross-tabulating trust towards the health center with educational level, no pattern was discernible.

The next table regards surveillance and big companies like Facebook or Google.

Table 4. Number and share of respondents who are concerned that big companies like Facebook or Google intrude into their private integrity on the Internet

	5 Agree	4	3	2	1 Do not agree	No opinion	Total
Number	93	42	44	22	78	44	323
%	29%	13%	13,5%	7%	24%	13,5%	
5 + 4; 2 + 1		42%		31%			
SoI*		46%		28%			

*SoI contains data from Internetstiftelsen 2019 for comparison [7].

There are no noteworthy differences between the results from the two surveys (and populations) in Table 4 above. This is interesting since there are differences when it comes to the following question regarding the Swedish state and authorities.

There are rather big differences between the results from the survey performed by Internetstiftelsen 2019 [7] and our survey results in the suburb, in Table 5. Respondents in the suburb are more concerned that the Swedish state and authorities intrude into their private integrity on the Internet, even if a larger share of the respondents in our survey report 1 Do not agree, than 5 Agree. In comparison with the results on the similar question about concern that big companies intrude, the numbers are similarly polarized.

Table 5. Number and share of respondents who are concerned that the Swedish state and authorities intrude into their private integrity on the Internet

	5 Agree	4	3	2	1 Do not agree	No opinion	Total
Number	70	45	49	24	96	39	323
%	22%	14%	15%	7%	30%	12%	
5 + 4; 2 + 1		36%		37%			
SoI*		21%		51%			

*SoI contains data from Internetstiftelsen 2019 for comparison [7].

3.2   Attitude Towards Digital Health Center and Other eHealth Questions

eHealth is partly about sharing of personal data. However, we do not know if respondents connect the Digital Health Center app with sharing of personal data or private integrity.

But it has to do with general trust. If users are not willing to share data with the app, then it could lead to a lower number of digital doctor's visits, it could be a clue into understanding the big difference in actual use of the eHealth app in Skäggetorp and the city center.

In Table 6, approximately half of the respondents reported 5 or 4 regarding if they can imagine using the Digital Health Center app. There was no illustration of the specific app and we cannot be sure whether respondents interpreted that the question specifically asked for the public sector app Digital Health Center and no other medical apps in general, for example private alternatives.

Table 6. Number and share of respondents who can imagine using the Digital Health Center app for contacts with doctors, nurses, and physiotherapists

	5 Agree	4	3	2	1 Do not agree	No opinion	Total
Number	106	40	32	22	63	18	281
%	38%	14,2%	11,4%	8%	22,4%	6%	

Results in the cross-tabulation shows that there are no major differences when it comes to sex regarding the question if the respondent could imagine using the app. Internetstiftelsen's survey [7] shows that females use such apps to a higher degree.

The older the age group the less they report imagining using the app. To keep in mind, most respondents belonged to the younger age groups. Of the respondents who reported their health status as "Very good" 60% choose alternative 5 or 4, while the share amongst the group that answers "Good" on health status, is lower when it comes to imagining using the app – 46%. Few respondents answered "Bad" or "Very bad" on the question about their health status. The older age groups report their health status as "Good" more frequently than "Very good". People with poor health status tend to need more health care.

When focusing on the three most reported ethnocultural/national backgrounds we see that Swedes are least likely to imagine using the app and Somalians most likely, nearly twice as likely, as the Swedes. At the same time, respondents who answered Swedish are more commonly found amongst the older age groups than people who reported Somalian. In this context we highlight that the sample was spontaneous in our survey, but the central government agency Statistics Sweden (www.scb.se) shows that in 2018 a significantly lesser share of people born in Africa (4%) are 65 years or older, in comparison with people born in Sweden (21%).

Respondents with an elementary school education or upper secondary school education are more likely to imagine using the app than respondents who started at or graduated from the university. Respondents who graduated from university are least likely. Most of the respondents reported that they have elementary school degree or upper secondary school degree, and some of the respondents reported that they have no schooling at all (and ended up answering the alternative "I don't know"). The number of respondents with academic degrees are rather few. Internetstiftelsen's survey [7] reports that level of education does not affect how many use such apps. However, respondents with lower level of education use other eHealth services (e.g. renewing medical recipe) to a lower degree than respondents with higher education. Regarding respondents' occupation, respondents searching for a job are slightly more likely to imagine using the app than students and respondents with employment. People who are at home with children are even more likely to imagine using the app. Retired persons are least likely, the same goes for early retirement/sick leave. At the same time, both groups probably need more health care than other respondents. Most respondents in the survey reported either working or studying as their main occupation.

Taken together 62% reported 5 or 4 on the question in Table 7. A person listed at the health center of Skäggetorp might not meet a doctor from that health center if using the Digital Health Center. Instead, the person has access to other doctors in the Region of Östergötland.

Table 7. Number and share of respondents who find it important to talk to the same staff at the Digital Health Center as they have met in real life at the health center?

	5 Agree	4	3	2	1 Do not agree	No opinion	Total
Number	117	56	30	19	32	27	281
%	42%	20%	10,5%	6,5%	11%	10%	

The last results we will present in this paper is from a question regarding usage of health or training apps.

Taken together 55% of respondents answer that they use a health or training app sometime, as shown in Table 8. However, the answer that was reported most frequently was Never (35,5%). According to Internetstiftelsen's survey respondents who are retired find using health/training apps least meaningful, while people with higher income find it most meaningful [7].

Table 8. Number and share who use health or training apps for monitoring and registering what you do at the Internet, e.g. monitoring your pulse or counting steps.

	Several times a day	Daily	Every week	Every month	Sometimes	Never	I don't know	Total
Number	34	43	23	13	44	100	24	281
%	12%	15%	8%	4,5%	16%	35,5%	9%	

4 Conclusions About Digital Inclusion and eHealth in the Suburb

The aim of this paper has been to explore digital participation and inclusion in the area of eHealth with a specific survey method in a Swedish suburb considered hard to survey.

We contribute by generating new data about use of digital services and attitudes amongst users that are usually difficult to reach by conventional survey studies such as residents of marginalized areas e.g. Swedish suburbs. eHealth has been described as requiring eHealth literacy that includes the ability to seek, find, understand, appraise, and use information from electronic sources for a health problem. The Digital Health Center app serves as a case of eHealth in this paper.

Our results show that digital participation and inclusion differs in our sample from a suburb, in comparison to results from the sample of Internetstiftelsen, and so too regarding the use of eHealth services. Our disaggregated data on use and attitude differs within and between age groups, sex, ethnicity, education, occupation, and health status. The statistics are descriptive and there are interesting findings regarding trust in health center and attitude towards the Digital Health Center. Groups that report high trust in the physical health center (elderly, Swedes) are also skeptical of the concept. Somalians and younger respondents report a lower trust towards the regular health center but have a more positive attitude towards the app. The relation between trust and attitude towards the app needs further exploration. If we take the call from the UN to get disaggregated data, age seems to be an important identity position. However, this does not explain why the usage of the app is low in Skäggetorp, the residents in the area does not have more elderly inhabitants than other areas in the Region of Östergötland. Neither can the low amount of digital doctor's visits be explained by the attitude towards the app since roughly 50% can imagine using it. The low usage is reflected in the low share of respondents who feel included in digital society. Because eHealth is a part of digital society and the ambition of wide inclusion for sustainable development, the non-use of eHealth services is a part of the digital divide. The low usage needs further exploration.

Then, what attitudes are expressed towards digital and eHealth services in the suburb? The results indicate that the sense of feeling part of digital society is a lot lower in comparison to Internetstiftelsen's survey and could be one clue. The respondents have physical access i.e. Smartphones, banking ID, even if it is lower than in general. A bit more than 50% of the respondents are motivated (i.e. could imagine using it). This raises questions about digital competence or/and eHealth literacy in terms of seeking, finding, understanding, and appraising information. It also raises questions about the requirements for increasing digital inclusion in eHealth, how much focus should be on increasing the digital competence of potential users versus efforts to develop eHealth services that fit a wider range of people with different competences and identity positions.

Future studies could explore the relationship between a trust, belonging, language, and eHealth – this is something that has been raised during the covid19 crisis. Another issue is to map the usage of private health apps in the suburb.

Acknowledgements. We are grateful to three anonymous reviewers who helped us improve the quality of the paper, and the research council Formas for the planning grant dnr 2018–02366.

References

1. van Dijk, J.: The Digital Divide. Polity, Cambridge (2020)

2. Gann, B.: Digital inclusion and health in wales. J. Consum. Health Internet **23**(2), 146–160 (2018)

3. Chesser, A., Burke, A., Reyes, J., Rohrberg, T.: Navigating the digital divide: a systematic review of eHealth literacy in underserved populations in the United States. Inform. Health Care **41**(1), 1–19 (2016)

4. Choi, N., DiNitto, D.: The digital divide among low-income homebound older adults: internet use patterns, eHealth literacy, and attitudes toward computer/Internet use. J. Med. Internet Res. **15**(5), e93 (2013)

5. Norman, C.D., Skinner, H.A.: eHealth literacy: essential skills for consumer health in a networked world. J. Med. Internet Res. **8**(2), 9 (2006)

6. Esaiasson, P.: Förorten: Ett samhällsvetenskapligt reportage. Stockholm, Timbro (2019)

7. Internetstiftelsen. https://svenskarnaochinternet.se/app/uploads/2019/10/svenskarna-och-int ernet-2019-a4.pdf. Accessed 12 Mar 2020

8. UN: Resolution 70/1. Transforming our world: the 2030 Agenda for Sustainable Development (2015)

9. Statistics Sweden: Statistisk uppföljning av Agenda 2030, SCB (2017)

10. Swedish Government: Hur Sverige blir bästa i världen på att använda digitaliseringens möjligheter – en skrivelse om politikens inriktning (2017)

11. Linköping Municipality. https://patientenkat.se/sv/resultat/Prim%C3%A4rv%C3%A5rd/ 2019. Accessed 16 Mar 2020

12. Novus: Vad tycker människorna som bor i Sveriges mest utsatta områden? En opinionsundersökning av Novus i Sveriges 61 mest utsatta områden (2018)

13. Gerdien, T.: Många som bor här har problem (2017). https://www.corren.se/nyheter/manga-som-bor-har-har-problem-om4558571.aspx. Accessed 05 Sept 2019

14. Region of Östergötland: Strategisk plan med treårsbudget 2020–2022 (2020)

15. Linköping Municipality: E-hälsostrategi 2017–2022 (2017)

16. Gustafsson, M., Elvström, R., Skill, K., Wihlborg, E.: DigidelCenter i Motala: Lärdomar för ökad digital kompetens. Arbetsmaterial LiU (2019)

17. Region Östergötland 2020 Statistiksammanställning: Primärvårdscentrum, Januari 2020

18. Cederberg, J.: Läkartidningen, Så mycket kostar digital vård 2018. http://www.lakartidningen. se/Aktuellt/Nyheter/2018/01/Sa-mycket-kostar-digital-vard/. Accessed 14 Mar 2020

19. Ebbers, W.E., Jansen, M.G.M., Johannes, A., van Deursen, A.M.: Impact of the digital divide on e-government: expanding from channel choice to channel usage. Gov. Inf. Q. **33**(4), 685–692 (2016)

20. Halperin, S., Heath, O.: Political Research: Methods and Practical Skills, 2nd edn. Oxford University Press, Oxford (2012)

21. Linköping Municipality. https://www.linkoping.se/kommun-och-politik/fakta-om-linkoping/ statistik/linkoping-i-siffror/befolkning/aldersstruktur/. Accessed 25 Mar 2020

22. Dawson, J.: Analysing Quantitative Survey Data for Business and Management Students. Sage, London (2017)

23. Burke, M., Oseni, T., Jolfaei, A., Gondal, I.: Cybersecurity indexes for eHeatlh. In: 12th Proceedings of Australian Conference on Health Informatics and Knowledge Management, pp 1–8. Macquarie University, Sydney, Australia (2018)

24. Askedal, K., Skiftenes, L., Abildsnes, E.: Reviewing effects of ICT in primary healthcare services: a public value perspective. In: The 23rd Americas Conference on Information Systems

"I'm Disabled and Married to a Foreign Single Mother". Public Service Chatbot's Advice on Citizens' Complex Lives

Linett Simonsen, Tina Steinstø, Guri Verne[✉], and Tone Bratteteig

University of Oslo, Gaustadalléen 23B, 0373 Oslo, Norway
{linetts,tinaste,guribv,tone}@ifi.uio.no

Abstract. This paper describes a study of citizens' chats with a chatbot of a public agency. We have analyzed chat logs and identified citizens' lack of domain knowledge as a source of inadequate or failed chatbot responses. We identify three types of lack of domain knowledge: lack of the right vocabulary, uncertainty if a regulation fits the citizen's situation or the "shape sorting box" problem, or citizen's misunderstanding the regulations. The most serious failure is when a misunderstanding is not detected and corrected during the chat. The chatbot we studied is not able to make sense of badly formed questions from citizens. As implications for design we suggest making the chatbot limitations visible by not presenting it as a human-like avatar with a name. We also suggest to enable domain knowledge learning through its conversations.

Keywords: Chatbot · Domain knowledge · Digitalization

1 Introduction

Governmental digitalization includes the digitalization of public administration as well as the digitalization of public services, which is where the citizens meet this change. Digitalized public services are often self-service solutions where the citizens have to carry out parts of the service, hence they need to know how to use the self-service solution. Use of electronic services could decrease the need for "administrative literacy" but will increase the need for computer skills [1]. The government in Norway is therefore concerned with the "digital competence" of the population since low or no digital competence in (parts of) the population may make the digital public services inaccessible to these citizens [2]. A digital divide rooted in inaccessible digital services may have severe socio-economic consequences for the affected individuals and for society [3]. Our concern in this paper is grounded in recent studies claiming that a major reason for unsuccessful or failed use of public self-services is the lack of domain knowledge [4–7]. These studies emphasize that an important service from public call centers and staffed offices is the ability of public administration advisors to "translate" questions from citizens into the right categories for the public "machinery" to process their inquiry. Being

© IFIP International Federation for Information Processing 2020
Published by Springer Nature Switzerland AG 2020
S. Hofmann et al. (Eds.): ePart 2020, LNCS 12220, pp. 133–146, 2020.
https://doi.org/10.1007/978-3-030-58141-1_11

able to use the self-services requires some understanding of the public service system [5]. In this paper we explore how a digitalized public service handles this problem by reporting from an empirical study of a particular public service where a chatbot has been designed to be the first public encounter for a citizen who seeks information and help [8]. The study gives an in-depth description of how the chatbot functions in practice through an analysis of a set of real chatbot conversations. The paper identifies problems occurring in practice that can act as a basis for designing improved digitalized public services.

The paper first presents the public service arrangements in Norway as well as the particular service where the chatbot has been introduced. We add a brief section about chatbots in general and this one in particular before we go on to tell about our study. We have analyzed logs from chatbot chats with citizens, and the next section describes three chats each illustrating a different type of problem concerned with lack of domain knowledge. The last section discusses what sort of domain knowledge the inquiries from the public may require; our analysis of the logs is confirmed by interview data. We also discuss how chatbots may handle the problems we have identified and hint to some implications for design. The last section concludes the paper.

2   Background: Digital Public Services in the Welfare State

The public service we have studied is a part of a welfare state, which offers a range of benefits and services for citizens in various life situations, e.g., retirement pension, unemployment allowance, healthcare services and sick leave benefits, a right to education, and various forms of family benefits. The benefits are allowances to the citizen based on legally grounded arrangements. In this paper, we concentrate on family benefits, because this is the services that the chatbot we have studied is made for. If a child is born in Norway, the mother of the child will automatically receive a birth allowance. Approx. two months after the child is born, she will start receiving a monthly child benefit (until the child is 18 years old). Single mothers and fathers, who live alone with children, may also be entitled to extended child benefit and infant supplement.

2.1   The Public Service

It is the Norway's Labour and Welfare Administration (LWA) that manages the services and benefits on behalf of the welfare state, altogether approx. 60 services and benefits. LWA meets the citizens through their 456 local offices, their Contact Center (CC) or through their digital services. The CC covers all services for the whole country and is responsible for contact with citizens through telephone, chat, and social media presence. Every year the center receives about 4.500.000 telephone calls, 700.000 written documents via net-based services (logged-in), and approx. 140.000 inquiries via chat and Facebook. The CC is not involved in the LWA's case handling: their employees only answer questions about rules and regulations, case handling response times, and payment dates. In addition, they can inform the citizen about status in her/his own case and teach citizens to use the web pages and self-service solutions.

As a part of its digitalization the LWA has expanded its digital communication and reduced the opening hours of the local offices. A chatbot has been introduced in the handling of inquiries about family benefits. A citizen who initiates a chat with LWA will first meet the chatbot before the chat can be transferred to a chat with a human. The chatbot is based on Machine Learning technology (ML) and LWA hopes that this technology combined with the large amounts of data captured by the public sector may enable automated services offering just-in-time welfare services to citizens without their active participation. The current chatbot is, however, not personal in that it does not require the citizen to log in or give any personal information.

Chatbots are expected to reduce the load on manned services, in particular calls to the call centers, by taking over the task of responding to questions from the citizens. Studying use of ML in the public sector is important for understanding how such technology functions in the public encounter [8].

2.2 Digitalization of the Public Encounter

The case handler or advisor, the street level bureaucrat who communicates directly with a citizen, represents the welfare state towards the citizens [9]. The digitalization of civil servants' work has implied that their contact with citizens and clients have changed from the "street level" contact [9], where they meet in person, to the "screen level", where data is entered into a screen, to the "system level", where decisions are made by a computer [10]. Several studies on channel choices and how they affect the relationship between the citizens and the government have been reported. Both Skaarup's study [11] of how different channels affect the citizens' feeling of control, and Ebbers et al.'s study [12] of how different channels are suitable for different purposes, show that the types of channel available can make a significant difference to the citizens. However, clients are increasingly being invited or forced to communicate with their advisors through online channels, but they also continue to use the traditional channels after adopting new digital service channels [13]. As digital technologies are used for larger parts of the communication between the client and the agency, new challenges arise. New types of skills are required from the citizen when manual services are replaced by electronic services.

There are a number of studies about what frontline service workers do and know, and many of them report that frontline service workers like the "street-level bureaucrats" [9] and the call center operators are good at "translating" callers' inquiries to internally specific categories and formats [14–16]. Several studies report that call center operators carry out knowledgeable and even emotional work in their response to a caller [17–23]. Flexible communication and emotional work are important for the operators to create a good interaction with the caller [17] and the ability to read a caller's emotional state can also be used for interpreting the emergency of the call [21].

There is a large variety of problems and issues that lead a citizen to call a public agency. Earlier studies have shown that many callers know the rules and regulations but ask if the rules apply to their particular situation; what Verne [6] calls "the shape-sorting box", i.e., fitting a real-life problem into one of the categories formed by the rules and regulations of the public agency. The callers need help to interpret the rules and understand how they fit their own life situation [6]. However, many callers show very little domain knowledge [5, 6]. The call advisors often need to disentangle the callers' problems into smaller steps that the callers can take themselves [24]. A study of call center operators in a public agency shows that the operators responded differently to different callers depending on how they interpreted the caller's digital competence and domain knowledge: A caller appearing helpless received more guidance and practical help than callers who expressed themselves in more competent ways [25].

3 Chatbots

A chatbot is an automatic system to which a user can text or "chat" in real time over the Internet [26]. Today, chatbots are able to communicate with people in natural language [27]. From the very first chatbot Eliza [28, 29], most chatbots have a limited vocabulary and repertoire based on preset keywords. The Eliza program first analyzed the syntax of the user's statement then formed a response from simple pattern recognition in addition to replacing keywords. Even if chatbots are able to "seemingly reply in intelligent ways to many queries, they still cannot understand a basic sentence in natural language" [30, 31]. Moreover, Hill et al. [31] found that users adapt their language by using simpler messages when interacting with a chatbot: the users they studied were very aware that they were communicating with a robot.

Today most chatbots are based on Machine Learning (ML), which is a special area within AI where statistical methods are used for identifying patterns in large data sets, to recognise patterns and produce results [32, 33]. ML is different from traditional programming where the machine performs predetermined operations. By being exposed to a number of examples or tasks with given answers, i.e., correct data, the machine is "trained". "Learning" is central in ML: the machine has to "be trained" by a set of training data and tested with a different set of test data [30, 32, 34]. The quality of the ML depends of the quality of the training data and the test data as well as how relevant these data sets are for the real data that the ML will meet when in operation. The algorithms will in principle give better results as the ML learns by processing more data. However, the development of a ML-based system like a chatbot needs to be monitored by people. A well-known example of a chatbot failure is the Microsoft chatbot Tay, which was designed to "learn" through dialogues with Twitter users and did not have security mechanisms to avoid "false teaching". Within 24 h Tay got out of control and had to be removed from the open net due to "trolling" from the Twitter users [35].

3.1 The LWA Chatbot

The LWA chatbot is named Anna (a pseudonym). Anna went public in the fall of 2018 and answered chats from approximately 400 users each day in the beginning of 2019. 40% of the users got an answer in this first encounter, 40% were transferred to chat with a human advisor, and 20% went to another channel (e.g., telephone) to communicate with LWA. Anna is not expected to respond to very complicated questions, as neither the technology nor the users are considered "good enough" yet.

Anna is based on ML technology and the aim is that it will learn and improve its responses through interactions with users. The ML analyses the users' questions to recognize what they are asking for. Once identified, the ML selects the corresponding response. ML is only used to identify questions: the answer the users receive to a question has been designed to adhere to the laws and regulations for that question, theme or keyword. The concrete formulation of the answers is designed by the advisors, who know what kind of replies the callers need to receive on particular questions.

In response to a question from a user, Anna pre-processes the text and classifies it as belonging to a category of questions, where all questions will match a predefined general answer. The ML performs several steps starting with correcting spelling errors and wrong words used. Then the ML identifies the question by trying to identify what the user wants to know by asking this question: the "intention" of this input. Based on the input the ML calculates which intention seems most probable. The system will match this intention with the set of predefined intentions. If the system finds the user's intention to be similar enough to a predefined intention, the predefined answer to this intention (i.e., question) will be given as the chat response. If the system does not find a sufficiently similar predefined intention, a standard fall-back message will be given, such as "Please rephrase your question in simpler terms".

Anna is constantly trained. LWA's chatbot trainers are constantly monitoring Anna, using reports generated by Anna in addition to reviewing chat conversations and feedback on Anna's performance from advisors. The chatbot trainers create training data based on this and run training sessions to improve Anna's responses. Training the chatbot means that more questions are classified, and new answers are added to the vocabulary of the system.

4 Method: Studying Chatbot Logs

The main material for this interpretive qualitative case study [36] is a segment of chat logs retrieved from chats between users and the LWA's chatbot Anna from more than 6 months in 2019, each week including approx. 3000 chats. For this study we extracted approximately 8000 unique chat logs from four of these weeks: two weeks in May and two weeks in September (more detailed studies in [37, 38]). We studied documents: LWA's plans and reports as well as the chatbot developers' documentation, and we interviewed and observed advisors and chatbot trainers at two CC's units. We carried out four semi-structured interviews with three different advisors in addition to observing them as they chatted with citizens. This gave us insight into typical questions and issues that the citizens ask about. We had three semi-structured interviews with two chatbot trainers working with Anna improvements, and observed them while they worked.

We took a hermeneutic approach [36] to analyzing the data, focusing on making sense of the log data. We used Suchman's analytical framework [39] as a starting point for interpreting and understanding chat logs where difficulties had occurred. The framework (see Fig. 1) distinguishes between the user's "actions available to the machine" (i.e. input) and actions not available to the machine, and the machine's response ("effects available to the user") as well as the machine's rationale or inner workings. In this paper we are concerned with the machine's responses to the users' actions and how Suchman's framework allows us to include the user's life circumstances, both those available and not available to the machine.

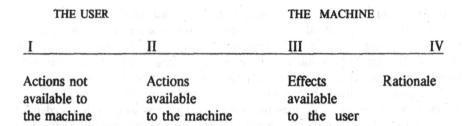

THE USER		THE MACHINE	
I	II	III	IV
Actions not available to the machine	Actions available to the machine	Effects available to the user	Rationale

Fig. 1. Suchman's analytical framework for studying and analyzing human-machine interaction [39].

We started by analyzing each chat to see if it was successful or not. We followed up the unsuccessful ones with a more detailed analysis of the questions and responses where we coded the challenges they illustrated into different categories. In this analysis we looked for communication breakdowns and used this as a basis for understanding how the chatbot worked. Examples that we considered difficult were discussed with chatbot trainers and advisors in the LWA. In the examples given below, the questions and answers are translated by us, taking care to preserve the nuances of the legal terminology and the user's original (mis)spelling.

5 Chatting with Anna

In the material we have analyzed we have found many chat logs that appear to have been successful: The user does not follow up with more questions, and our interpretation of Anna's answer indicates that it is correct and relevant. LWA's criteria for a successful answer from Anna is a "sufficient" answer, where the chatbot gives relevant and correct information as a response to the user input.

Some of the chat logs indicate an unsuccessful chat session. In some obvious cases, the user leaves the chat after swearing or expressing dissatisfaction with Anna's responses, e.g., by writing "This is hopeless" before leaving. In other chats, the user does not express dissatisfaction but leaves the chat abruptly. In this section we present and discuss three examples of chat conversations that illustrate different challenges to the use of chatbots in a legal setting. We focus on lack of domain knowledge as a reason for lack of success, i.e., chat conversations where a user applies the wrong word or inconsistent terms or shows lack of knowledge about the rules and regulations. In the following three subsections, we present different chat sessions that illustrate how weak domain knowledge of the user leads to challenges in getting good answers.

5.1 Lack of Key Concept

In this category, the user formulates a question where the wrong terms are used. In this example the user asks a question about the amount of child benefit and writes the word "*child benefit*" (translated from Norwegian with the misspelling preserved). Despite the spelling mistake, Anna recognizes that the question is about child benefits. Anna does, however, not recognize that the user asks about the amount.

Anna: My name is Anna and I am a chatbot.
Anna: I am best adapted to answering short questions. Remember to include what type of benefit you are asking about.
Anna: How can I help you?
Anna: For English chat, click here *(button)*
User: What is the child bennefit* this year?
Anna: If you have a child under the age of 18 living with you in Norway, you may be entitled to child benefit.
Anna: You can receive child benefit from the month after the child is born.
Anna: If you are entitled to child benefit at a later point, you may receive child benefit from the month after the terms have been met.
Anna: Child benefit will be paid up until the month before the child turns 18. If the right to child benefit ceases earlier than this, you will receive child benefit up until the month the terms ceases to apply.
• Who is entitled to child benefit? *(button)*

• Extended child benefit *(button)*
• Payment *(button)*
• Changes in family situation *(button)*
• Apply for child benefit *(button)*
User: What is the rate of the child benefit?
Anna: Ordinary child benefit is 1054 NOK monthly per child.
Anna: Extended child benefit is 1054 NOK and will be in addition to the child benefit you will receive for children living with you.
Anna: Infant supplement is 660 NOK
• Extended child benefit *(button)*
• Infant supplement *(button)*
User: Thank you, Anna ☺
Anna: You are welcome!
Conversation continues ...

*misspelled word
(Conversation ID: *617631 (masked code)*)

This user seems to understand that the first term s/he uses does not give the wanted answer and tries to rephrase the question using the term "rate". The user gets a different answer, which s/he seems to be satisfied with.

5.2   The "Shape-Sorting" Box

In this category, Anna cannot link the user's question to the relevant services and benefits this user asks for. The result is that Anna does not recognize what the user asks for, and therefore cannot help.

Anna: My name is Anna and I am a chatbot
Anna: I am best adapted to answering short questions. Remember to include what type of benefit you are asking about.
Anna: How can I help you?
Anna: For English chat, click here *(button)*
User: Going to have a child, what do I need to apply for?
Anna: I'm sorry, but I don't understand what you are asking.
Anna: I will understand it better if you write short questions and which benefit it is regarding.
Anna: Can you ask the question again?

• Need more help *(button)*
• No (button)
User: How do I receive money when I am expecting a child?
Anna: Which day the payment arrives, depends on which benefit (it regards).
Anna: You can see your payments from LWA at "Your payments" at <LWA.website>, but they do not show up before they have arrived in your account.
<lists info about payments>

(Conversation ID: *679785*)

The question formulated by the user in this example indicates weak domain knowledge, as the user does not know what the different services and benefits are called, or who is entitled to what. We call this a problem with "the shape-sorting box": matching a citizen's life situation to the various services and benefits.

The user leaves the chat without asking further questions. If this user had asked explicitly to be transferred to chat with an advisor, it would have been visible in the chat log. S/he may have changed the contact to another channel or given up without the chat log giving any indication.

5.3   A Logical/Legal Flaw

In this category, the terms used indicate a weak understanding of the rules and regulations for LWA's benefits and services. In this chat, the user asks the question "can a young disabled person married to a foreign single mother receive child benefit and child supplement". The question contains the legally inconsistent phrase "married to a ... single mother": the rules are that if you are married you are not categorized as a single parent. Anna's response concerns benefit for single parents, which does not match the user's stated life situation. The user follows up with asking whether a "foreign single mother" can receive child benefit and child supplement. Anna does not recognize that the user expresses a legal inconsistency and responds by providing more information about the rights of single parents.

Anna: My name is Anna and I am a chatbot.
Anna: I am best adapted to answering short questions. Remember to include what type of benefit you are asking about.
Anna: How can I help you?
Anna: For English chat, click here *(button)*
User: can a young disabled person married to a foreign single mother receive child benefit and child supplement
Anna: If you are a single mother or father, you may be entitled to extended child benefit if you are living alone with children.
Anna: The extended child benefit is child benefit for one more child than what you actually are living together with.
Anna: You have to apply for an extended child benefit, it will not be automatically granted.
• Who is entitled to child benefit? *(button)*
<lists info about extended benefit>
User: Entitled to extended child benefit? *(action)*
Anna: If you are a single mother or father you can receive extended benefit if you are living alone with the child and:
• you are separated, divorced or widowed
<continues to list criteria for extended benefit>
Anna: If you do not have common children with the person you are living with, we do not need documentation that you are not living together. It could be:
• Declaration of breakup
• Separation permit
• When does the right to extended child benefit expire? *(button)*
• Apply for extended child benefit *(button)*
• Shared child benefit *(button)*
User: When does the right to extended child benefit cease? *(action)*
Anna: Extended child benefit will cease if:
• You marry
• You have children with a new cohabitant
• You have been cohabitant with a person you do

not have joint children with for twelve months
• You move together with the father of the child
User: can a foreign single mother receive child benefit and child supplement
Anna: If you are a single mother or father, you may be entitled to extended child benefit if you are living alone with children.
Anna: <lists criteria for extended benefit>
User: Payment *(action)*
Anna: Child benefit will be paid out the last day of the week each month. Child benefit is not liable to tax.
Anna: Remember that you can see your payments from LWA by logging into 'Your LWA'.
Anna: At <LWA.website> you can find an overview of payment dates for child benefit.
<lists payment info>
User: Can foreign single mother receive child supplement
Anna: In some cases, the mother may receive the entire period of child benefit
Anna: She can be alone with the care or live together with the child's other parent that have not yet served up the right to child benefit.
• I am caring for the child alone *(button)*
• I live together with the father/co-mother *(button)*
• I mean child benefit *(button)*
• I mean transitional benefit *(button)*
User: I mean child benefit *(action)*
Anna: If you are a single mother or father, you may be entitled to extended child benefit if you are living alone with children.
Anna: The extended child benefit is child benefit for one more child than what you actually are living together with.
Anna: You have to apply for an extended child benefit, it will not be automatically granted.
<lists info about extended benefit>

(Conversation ID: *670860*)

Nowhere in this conversation does Anna explain that you cannot be categorized as a single mother if you are married. As the user continues to ask about benefits for single mothers, this misunderstanding is not detected, and Anna continues to answer about benefits for single mothers without explaining that the mother in question may not be eligible for such benefits. The user selects the button "I mean child benefit" and is given a response that Anna has already provided earlier in the conversation. Since Anna's reply contains the buttons "I mean child benefit" and "I mean transitional benefit", it may look as if the system recognizes the user's weak domain knowledge. However, the answers the user receives may be completely irrelevant if the mother in question actually is married. In the worst case, this user is misled by the chatbot into believing that the mother he is married to is eligible for benefits for single mothers, which she is not.

6   Discussion

6.1   Chatbots as a Frontline in Public Services

Previous research about call centers has shown that the operators do more than merely answer questions about facts and information. The operators' expertise and knowledge about their work add value to their clients' inquiries [19]. Whalen et al. [23] describe operators' work by the seemingly contradictory notions of improvisation and chore-ography, indicating that their work routines are craft-like practices where the operator adjusts his/her response to the situation-at-hand: the actual, concrete inquiry from the client. Verne's study of call center operators in a public agency showed that operators helped callers to formulate their inquiries in the relevant and correct terms as well as providing problem-solving steps that the caller could perform to solve the problem [25].

There is no creative translation capacity in a chatbot: the chatbot only compares the words given to it through the user's input and matches these to the predefined keywords – the only pre-processing done by the chatbot is spell check. The cases above show that the chatbot often does not forgive spelling errors or use of wrong words by clients. This makes the chatbot a very strict first encounter with the welfare agency for many citizens. The chatbot becomes a representative for LWA, hence the welfare state may appear rigid when it does not provide information that the citizen is not aware of that s/he should ask for.

6.2   Domain Knowledge

Our study shows different ways that the lack of domain knowledge affects the citizens conversations with the welfare state through chatbots. We have identified three types of domain knowledge that may result in unsuccessful communication with chatbots like Anna if missing.

The first type of domain knowledge is the language: the correct terms. The user in our first case misspells a (correct) term and also uses an everyday word ("amount") that Anna does not recognize. Lack of knowledge about the correct terms is a well-documented problem that goes deeper as knowledge about the correct terms often depends on knowl-edge about the phenomenon that the terms refer to, i.e., the rules and regulations of the public service. Our interviews with advisors confirmed that many citizens contact them using everyday language. "It is easier for them to use the chat and say 'Hi, I am new in this. And I wonder about so-and-so'. Maybe they don't know where to start. These are the people I think contact us on the chat," said one of the advisors. Another advisor confirmed this by stating that "My experience is that many people ask like 'Hi, I plan to have kids, my due date is soon, my due date will be like so-and-so. What should I take care of? How do I apply?'" The tax call advisors in Verne's study [6] recognize weak domain knowledge by wrong or inconsistent terms used by the callers. A study among immigrants in Norway showed that even if they had lived in Norway for several decades and spoke Norwegian well, the specific terms of LWA were difficult to understand and master because the terms had no equivalents in their mother tongue [40]. This also holds for native Norwegians without competence in LWA's services: the advisors told that they "normally use an oral language style to make it easier to understand for the users" in the chats and that they "break the information down to make it more understandable". Another advisor told us that "it is very rare that you can use the standard answers", so the answers have to be adjusted. "I assess every chat and adjust the information not too much and not too little to the concrete chat." Moreover, the advisors emphasized that the users ask in many different ways: "There are incredibly many nuances and incredibly many ways of solving things".

The second type of domain knowledge also seems to be a language problem, but we categorize it as a "shape sorting box" problem. The user asks if s/he is eligible for a particular benefit. This problem is discussed by Verne [6]. Her study of the tax authorities' call center concluded that many of the callers asked how their particular life situation fitted with the rules – even callers with good knowledge about the rules wanted to have their interpretation of the laws and regulations confirmed from the official view of the tax authorities. This was supported by the advisors: "Very often they want a confirmation because it is complicated regulations and many nuances" and "the users contact us to make sure they have done things right". The advisors also said that "much of the information [the users ask for] you can find at the <LWA.website>, but we understand that they chat with us. Because it is a lot of information. And they have read it, but they have not really understood it properly". They also say that "The application [for benefits] has become a lot easier, but people don't stop contacting the LWA". One advisor explained that "A challenge in LWA is that things overlap a lot. There are no strict borders, parental things flow into [other topics] … There are a lot of terminologies that are similar, but not quite the same, but almost the same: child benefit, child allowance …". Anna is not able to answer questions about the "shape sorting box" because the chatbot only answers general questions, referring to general rules and regulations. Anna helps people find general information but cannot relate to the actual situation of a person.

The third type of domain knowledge is a misunderstanding of the rules that looks like a "shape sorting box" question. However, as the chatbot does not detect this misunderstanding, there is a danger of mis-informing the caller, who may get an unpleasant surprise if s/he has calculated with a benefit it later turns out that s/he is not entitled to. The advisors told us that "Many people do not understand what is written at <LWA.website>". Combined with what the advisors told about adjustment of their language to the individual user and the many nuances in both questions and answers, we find that the human chat offers what call centers normally do: "I answer on their level".

6.3 Implications for Design

In this study, we have found several challenges in citizens' chat with Anna that suggest shifting the focus in chatbot design from a focus on the chatbot end of the interaction to taking the whole chat conversation into consideration (in line with [26, 41, 43]). Our analysis of the chatbot's responses to the users' questions (cf. Fig. 1, [39]) has of course made use of our (human) interpretation of the content of the questions and what they mean as well as the assumed value and appropriateness of the chatbot's answers. Based on this analysis we suggest some implications for the design of the chatbot end of those conversations. As users' lack of domain knowledge may cause miscommunication and communication breakdowns, we encourage chatbot designers to explore the possibility of helping users gain domain knowledge, for instance by providing cues or basic domain information as part of the chatbot communication.

Our analysis indicates that users' expectations were out of step with the practical realities of chatbot capabilities, causing frustration and dissatisfaction on the user side. One reason for the high expectations may be that LWA's chatbot Anna is presented with a human name and a human-like avatar. The chatbot logs we studied contained anthropomorphic trigger responses such as "Aww, now you are making me blush" and "I understand very well what you are saying". Our analysis suggests that not all users understand that they communicate with a computer, and we suggest designing the chatbot in a way that does not try to impersonate a human, but clearly reveal its non-human qualities. Programmed trigger responses may set unrealistic expectations framing the ongoing user experience [17, 27, 42], hence we suggest a careful approach when implementing such features.

Reflecting on the introduction of Anna, one of the advisors say that "It has been a pronounced change – there are fewer conversations on [the human] chat but I do not know if more people get help". As of today, LWA's chatbot can only be used as a non-logged in service. However, it is possible to imagine a future were users can communicate with the chatbot as logged in users. In this case the system may have access to personal information about the users, e.g., if they are married or have children. This may affect how the chatbot system will be able to help users in their particular situations. The chatbot can, e.g., check if the marital status mentioned in the question is in line with what is registered in their databases and respond appropriately.

The fact that the chat is the first encounter with the welfare state for the citizen makes it important that the chatbot's answers are to be trusted. We saw a small sign that the trust is fragile in a chat conversation with a human, where the user asks a question and the human chat advisor recommends a form and provides the link to the form. The user responds by asking "Is the form you linked to the right one?" The advisor had to explain the reasons for recommending this particular form. Chatbot encounters that make users lose trust in the welfare state may be a serious cost of the benefits of digitalization.

7 Concluding Remarks

In this paper we have explored how a digitalized public service in the form of a chatbot handles citizens' inquiries about family benefits. By analyzing logs from chatbot chats with citizens we have shown that chats where citizens lack domain knowledge may result in inadequate responses by the chatbot. Lack of domain knowledge is exemplified as lack of the right vocabulary, uncertainty if a regulation fits the citizen's situation – the "shape sorting box" problem, or misunderstanding the regulations. We find that the lack of adequate response from the chatbot is particularly problematic if a misunderstanding that the citizen has is not detected and addressed during the chat. Our studies of real chats with a chatbot show that the chatbot is not able to interpret and "translate" badly formed questions from citizens into the right categories for further advancement of their inquiry. We suggest making the limitations of the chatbot's capabilities more visible by presenting it as a computer rather than a human-like avatar as well as expanding its ability to explain and teach citizens relevant domain knowledge through its conversations. Lack of domain knowledge makes the user unaware of inconsistencies and limitations in the chatbot's answers.

Acknowledgements. We thank LWA Contact Center and its leader for giving us access to the chat logs and for allowing us to interview the advisors and chatbot trainers.

References

1. Grönlund, Å., Hatakka, M., Ask, A.: Inclusion in the e-service society – investigating administrative literacy requirements for using e-services. In: Wimmer, M.A., Scholl, J., Grönlund, Å. (eds.) EGOV 2007. LNCS, vol. 4656, pp. 216–227. Springer, Heidelberg (2007). https://doi.org/10.1007/978-3-540-74444-3_19
2. Carretero, S., Vuorikari, R., Punie, Y.: The digital competence framework for citizens. Publications Office of the European Union (2017)
3. Van Deursen, A.J., Van Dijk, J.A.: The first-level digital divide shifts from inequalities in physical access to inequalities in material access. New Media Soc. **21**(2), 354–375 (2019)
4. Breit, E., Salomon, R.: Making the technological transition – citizens' encounters with digital pension services. Soc. Policy Adm. **49**, 299–315 (2014)
5. Madsen, C.Ø., Kræmmergaard, P.: The efficiency of freedom: single parents' domestication of mandatory e-government channels. Gov. Inf. Q. **32**(4), 380–388 (2015)
6. Verne, G.: The winners are those who have used the old paper form. On citizens and automated public services. Doctoral dissertation, Department of Informatics, University of Oslo (2015)
7. Verne, G., Bratteteig, T.: Do-it-yourself services and work-like chores: on civic duties and digital public services. Pers. Ubiquit. Comput. **20**(4), 517–532 (2016). https://doi.org/10.1007/s00779-016-0936-6
8. Lindgren, I., Madsen, C.Ø., Hofmann, S., Melin, U.: Close encounters of the digital kind: a research agenda for the digitalization of public services. Gov. Inf. Q. **36**(3), 427–436 (2019)
9. Lipsky, M.: Street-Level Bureaucracy. Dilemmas of the Individual in Public Service. Russel Sage, New York (2010)
10. Bovens, M., Zouridis, S.: From street-level to system-level bureaucracies: how information and communication technology is transforming administrative discretion and constitutional control. Public Adm. Rev. **62**, 174–184 (2002)
11. Skaarup, S.: The Mediation of Authority. In: SCSS.TCD.IE, pp. 1–32 (2012)
12. Ebbers, W.E., Pieterson, W.J., Noordman, H.N.: Electronic government: rethinking channel management strategies. Gov. Inf. Q. **25**(2), 181–201 (2008)
13. Madsen, C.Ø., Hofmann, S., Pieterson, W.: Channel choice complications. In: Lindgren, I., Janssen, M., Lee, H., Polini, A., Rodríguez Bolívar, M.P., Scholl, H.J., Tambouris, E. (eds.) EGOV 2019. LNCS, vol. 11685, pp. 139–151. Springer, Cham (2019). https://doi.org/10.1007/978-3-030-27325-5_11

14. Wynn, E: Office conversation as an information medium. Doctoral dissertation, University of California, Department of Anthropology, Berkeley (1979)
15. Suchman, L., Wynn, E.: Procedures and problems in the office. Office Technol. People **2**, 133–154 (1984)
16. Bowker, G.C., Star, S.L.: Sorting Things Out: Classification and Its Consequences. MIT, Cambridge (1999)
17. Maass, S., Rommes, E.: Uncovering the invisible: gender-sensitive analysis of call center work and software. In: Zorn, I., Maass, S., Rommes, E., Schirmer, C., Schelhowe, H. (eds.) Gender Designs IT. VS Verlag für Sozialwissenschaften, Wiesbaden (2007). https://doi.org/10.1007/978-3-531-90295-1_6
18. Martin, D., O'Neill, J., Randall, D., Rouncefield, M.: How can I help you? Call centres, classification work and coordination. J. CSCW **16**(3), 231–264 (2007). https://doi.org/10.1007/s10606-007-9045-4
19. Muller, M.J.: Invisible work of telephone operators: an ethnocritical analysis. J. CSCW **8**(1–2), 31–61 (1999). https://doi.org/10.1023/A:1008603223106
20. Nyberg, D.: Computers, customer service operatives and cyborgs: intra-actions in call centres. Organ. Stud. **30**(11), 1181–1199 (2009)
21. Svensson, M.: Routes, routines and emotions in decision making of emergency call takers. Doctoral dissertation, School of Management, Blekinge Institute of Technology (2012)
22. Tjora, A.H.: The technological mediation of the nursing-medical boundary. Sociol. Health Illn. **22**(6), 721–741 (2000)
23. Whalen, J., Whalen, M., Henderson, K.: Improvisational choreography in teleservice work. Br. J. Sociol. **53**(2), 239–258 (2002)
24. Bratteteig, T., Verne, G.: Conditions for autonomy in the information society; disentangling as a public service. Scand. J. Inf. Syst. **24**, 51–71 (2012)
25. Verne, G.: Two faces of autonomy: learning from non-users of an e-service. Syst. Signs Actions **8**(1), 6–24 (2014)
26. Brandtzaeg, P., Følstad, A.: Chatbots: changing user needs and motivations. Interactions **25**(5), 38–43 (2018)
27. Liao, Q.V., et al.: All work and no play? Conversations with a question-and-answer chatbot in the wild. In: CHI 2018, Montreal, QC, Canada, pp. 3.1–3.13 (2018)
28. Weizenbaum, J.: Computer Power and Human Reason: From Judgment to Calculation. Freeman, San Francisco (1976)
29. Shevat, A.: Designing Bots: Creating Conversational Experience. O'Reilly Media Inc, Beijing (2017)
30. Holmquist, L.E.: Intelligence on tap: artificial intelligence as a new design material. Interactions **24**(4), 28–33 (2017)
31. Hill, J., Ford, W.R., Farreras, I.G.: Real conversations with artificial intelligence: a comparison between human–human online conversations and human–chatbot conversations. Comput. Hum. Behav. **49**, 245–250 (2015)
32. Jordan, M.I., Mitchell, T.M.: Machine learning: trends, perspectives, and prospects. Science **349**(6245), 255–260 (2015)
33. Russell, S., Norvig, P.: Artificial Intelligence: A Modern Approach. Pearson, Boston (2010)
34. Broussard, M.: Artificial Unintelligence: How Computers Misunderstand the World. MIT Press, Cambridge (2018)
35. Hendler, J., Mulvehill, A.: Social Machines: The Coming Collision of Artificial Intelligence, Social Networking, and Humanity (1st). Apress, Berkeley (2016)
36. Myers, M.D.: Qualitative Research in Business & Management, 2nd edn. Sage Publications, Thousand Oaks (2013)

37. Simonsen, L.: Når brukerdialogen automatiseres – hva blir vanskelig? En kvalitativ studie av sekvensen av handlinger mellom menneske og chatbot. Master thesis, Department of Informatics, University of Oslo (2019)
38. Steinstø, T.: Bruk av chatbot i praksis. En kvalitativ studie av utfordringer ved bruk av chatbot i offentlige tjenester. Master thesis, Department of Informatics, University of Oslo (2020)
39. Suchman, L.: Human-Machine Reconfigurations: Plans and Situated Actions, 2nd edn. Cambridge UP, Cambridge (2007)
40. Nguyen, T.H.: Jeg blir så sliten i tankene. Innvandreres bruk av offentlige nettbaserte tjenester. Master thesis, Department of Informatics, University of Oslo (2019)
41. Hageback, N.: The Virtual Mind: Designing the Logic to Approximate Human Thinking. CRC Press, Boca Raton (2017)
42. Luger, E., Sellen, A.: Like having a really bad PA: the Gulf between user expectation and experience of conversational agents. In: CHI 2016, pp. 5286–5297 (2016)
43. Følstad, A., Brandtzæg, P.B.: Chatbots and the new world of HCI. Interactions **24**(4), 38–42 (2017)

Author Index

Printed in the United States
By Bookmasters